HOUSEPLANTS
for Beginners

Quarto.com

© 2023 Quarto Publishing Group USA Inc.
Text © 2017 Quarto Publishing Group USA Inc.

First Published in 2023 by New Shoe Press, an imprint of The Quarto Group,
100 Cummings Center, Suite 265-D, Beverly, MA 01915, USA.
T (978) 282-9590 F (978) 283-2742

Essential, In-Demand Topics, Four-Color Design, Affordable Price
New Shoe Press publishes affordable, beautifully designed books covering evergreen, in-demand subjects. With a goal to inform and inspire readers' everyday hobbies, from cooking and gardening to wellness and health to art and crafts, New Shoe titles offer the ultimate library of purposeful, how-to guidance aimed at meeting the unique needs of each reader. Reimagined and redesigned from Quarto's best-selling backlist, New Shoe books provide practical knowledge and opportunities for all DIY enthusiasts to enrich and enjoy their lives.

Visit Quarto.com/New-Shoe-Press for a complete listing of the New Shoe Press books.

New Shoe Press titles are also available at discount for retail, wholesale, promotional, and bulk purchase. For details, contact the Special Sales Manager by email at specialsales@quarto.com or by mail at The Quarto Group, Attn: Special Sales Manager, 100 Cummings Center, Suite 265-D, Beverly, MA 01915, USA.

10 9 8 7 6 5 4 3 2 1

ISBN: 978-0-7603-8390-2
eISBN: 978-0-7603-8391-9

The content in this book was previously published in *Houseplants: The Complete Guide to Choosing, Growing, and Caring for Indoor Plants* (Cool Springs Press 2017) by Lisa Eldred Steinkopf.

Library of Congress Cataloging-in-Publication Data available

Photography: Chelsea Steinkopf; also Lori Adams, GAP photos, iStock, Crystal Liepa, and Shutterstock.com.

Printed in China

HOUSEPLANTS
for Beginners

A Simple Guide for New Plant Parents for Making Houseplants Thrive

LISA ELDRED STEINKOPF

NEW SHOE PRESS

Contents

Introduction

We all have the need to nurture and care for other living things. Maybe you aren't ready for a cat, dog, or fish, but bringing home a houseplant can fulfill that need. Place a plant on the windowsill and it will add living beauty to your home. Wake up every day and it will greet you as it cleans the air and improves your mood. Houseplants ask for so little but add so much life to a home. The care of that green friend falls solely on the owner. Being successful in that undertaking is important, so our hope is this book can help you keep your green roommate alive, healthy, and vibrant.

There is no such thing as a natural green thumb. Many believe either you are born with one or not. The claim of having a brown or black thumb has had many dead plants placed at its doorstep. Yet having a green thumb is just a matter of paying attention to the needs of your plants and noticing when they are trying to tell you something. Killing a plant or two (or more) is not a crime, and can be a good learning experience. Don't be discouraged, as growing beautiful plants is easy if you have the time and pay attention to their specific needs, and this book will show you how to do that.

Time restraints are another popular excuse as to why someone has no plants in their home. One easy plant can take less than five minutes a week to care for, and the benefits it brings will lead to a desire for more greenery in your life. Having plants continually die leads to frustration and possibly plastic plants. Not acceptable. When a few key components such as lighting preference, water, and placement are understood and correctly executed, your plants will thrive. Liking and being successful with plants has more rewards than are always apparent. Plants have been proven to clean the air around us. B. C. Wolverton, a NASA scientist, conducted many experiments in the 1980s and found that plants remove VOCs—volatile organic chemicals—from our indoor environments. These chemicals can come from carpet, paint, manufactured furniture, household cleaning products, and more. One plant can remove most of the VOCs from a 100-square-foot area.

An important aspect of owning houseplants is the undeniable therapy that caring for plants affords us. In this uncertain, sometimes scary, fast-paced world, slowing down to care for something that is dependent on us can be therapeutic. Pick up a plant, remove dead leaves, check the growing medium for water, and wash the leaves with a soft cloth or sponge. Move quietly from plant to plant, or maybe you prefer to sing, hum, or talk to your plants. No judgment here. One plant may become many more when the time it takes to care for one plant isn't enough to untangle the knots from the day. Many professional people own large collections of plants for just this reason. Working with their plants takes them away from the enormous stress of their jobs. As Elvin McDonald wrote in his book *Plants as Therapy*, "I believe that plants have enormous potential for maintaining emotional stability and . . . improving the lives of human beings." Nothing truer can be said.

Quite often, if you have a problem with a houseplant, you search online for information and help. But not every piece of information floating around on the Internet is true or pertinent to the specific plant for which you are caring. The information in this book will dispel the myths and misinformation about successfully raising houseplants. Plant societies are another good source of information. If you wish to learn as much as you can about a family of plants, such as cacti and other succulents, orchids, or African violets, join a plant society in your area. The people in these clubs have usually been growing those plants for a long time. Nothing beats the hands-on knowledge of people who have successfully grown a family of plants. Because they love their plants, they are more than willing to share their expertise. They want you to succeed with your plants. Besides, it is a wonderful way to interact with people. Joining a plant group can help you find like-minded people who don't tune out when you talk nonstop about your plants.

I hope the information in this book will give you the confidence you need to bring a plant or two home to improve your environment and give it a warmer, more comfortable feeling that will bring joy to those who enter. You may find that almost before you know it, people entering your home will comment, "It's like a jungle in here!" Is that a bad thing? I think not. It is a good thing!

Planting

In every houseplant owner's life, the time comes to get your hands dirty. Plants grow, increase in size, and eventually need to be moved to a new container. In certain situations, it may mean the plant is moved into a similar-size container, returned to the same container, or moved into a larger container.

This process is one that can be enjoyable, knowing that you are helping your plant grow better. Providing it with the best potting medium for its particular needs ensures the root system can function well and provide the plant with what it requires for optimal growth.

Repotting or up-potting are easy tasks, if done correctly and at the right time for the plant. Assess the needs of the plant you are working with. Is it root-bound? Is it looking undernourished or off-color? Does it need a new, clean pot or a different color pot to match your décor? Keep in mind the size container you need for your plant when shopping for a new pot. Measuring the old container to determine the size needed before purchasing a new one can be helpful. If up-potting a plant, make sure this is being done at a time when the plant is actively growing. The plant will show you its thanks by pushing out new, healthy growth.

POTTING SUPPLIES

Before getting started, make sure all the supplies you may need are at hand.

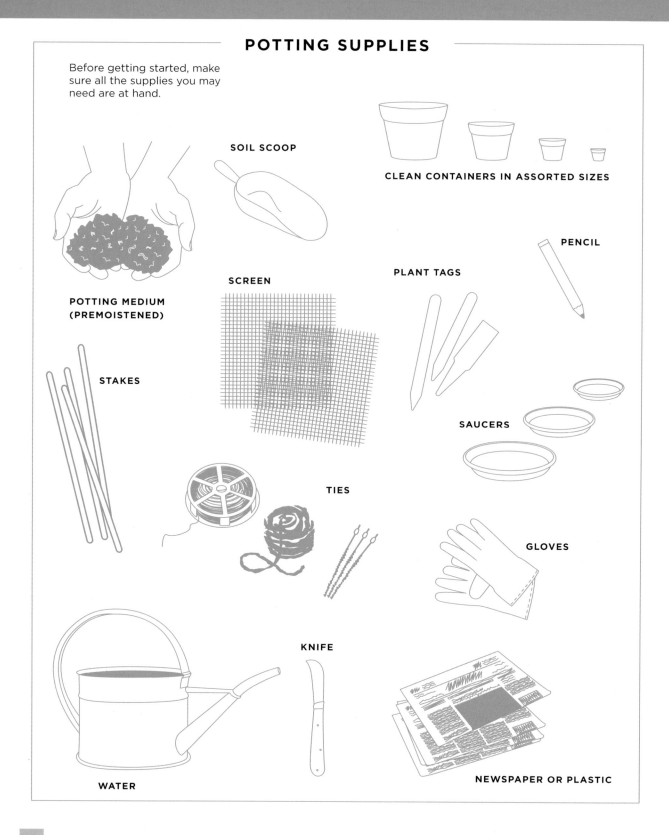

SOIL SCOOP

CLEAN CONTAINERS IN ASSORTED SIZES

PENCIL

POTTING MEDIUM (PREMOISTENED)

SCREEN

PLANT TAGS

STAKES

SAUCERS

TIES

GLOVES

KNIFE

WATER

NEWSPAPER OR PLASTIC

This *Pilea involucrate* 'Norfolk' is residing in its utilitarian grower's pot and will be moved into the decorative pot on the right.

When up-potting, only change to a pot the next size up, unless the plant is extremely root-bound. You may well up-pot a plant many times during its lifetime.

Repotting and Up-Potting

Repotting most often involves moving a newly purchased plant from the utilitarian grower's pot to a more decorative pot of the same size. Inspect the roots when repotting: If the pot is full of roots and seems root-bound, you may have to repot in a larger container. Also, check that the depth of the plant in the potting medium is correct. Quite often, the stems are buried in ½ to 1 inch of extra soil. Remove the superfluous soil and pot the plant at a better depth. Repotting is also necessary if your pot gets broken or you notice an accumulation of salt residue on the pot rim.

If your container has broken or a fertilizer salt residue has built up on it, changing pots—not changing the size—can become necessary.

This ZZ plant, *Zamioculcas zamiifolia*, has filled the container with roots and is unable to grow successfully any longer.

When up-potting, or moving your plant to a larger container, do it gradually. If you are moving a plant from a 4-inch pot, move up to a 6-inch pot, a 6-inch pot to an 8-inch pot, and so on. Moving a plant to a much larger pot can cause problems. If a plant has too much soil surrounding its rootball, it may cause the roots to rot, as they cannot use all the water available to them.

What are some of the indicators your plant needs to be up-potted? One of the most obvious is your plant is top-heavy. If your plant starts to dry down, it may topple over because the plant is heavier than the pot, soil, and water in the soil combined. Find a more proportionate container, making sure you do not choose a container too large for your plant. If your plant isn't root-bound, it may be that you need to choose a heavier container, such as one made of clay or ceramic, which will better support your plant.

◀ The roots have grown through the holes in the bottom of the pot. To successfully remove the plant, it may be necessary to cut the roots off.

▲ The pot may have to be cut away from the roots to enable the plant to be removed from the pot. If it is a clay pot, the plant may have to be cut out or the pot broken.

The ZZ plant, *Zamioculcas zamiifolia*, has been up-potted to a larger container that will allow the plant to spread its roots and grow more successfully.

The fiddle leaf fig had roots showing at the top and so soil was added.

If, when you water your plant, the water sits on top of the medium and takes excessive time to run out of the drainage hole, it may be a sign the medium is broken down and compacted. Medium decomposes in the container and can become compacted over time, not leaving enough air spaces for the water to run through. This isn't healthy for the plant and it may need a larger pot, but at the very least, fresh medium.

On the flip side, the water may run out the bottom of the pot so quickly that it may not be moistening the soil at all. If a plant dries out completely, the medium may shrink away from the sides of the container, leaving a gap. This usually happens to a medium that is composed mostly of peat moss. It will either need to be up-potted or rectified by dunking the whole pot into a receptacle of water and allowing it to rehydrate and expand.

If your plant wilts and you need to water it more often, it may need larger living quarters. Check the bottom of the container for roots protruding from the drainage holes. If this is the case, it needs to be up-potted. After removing the plant from its pot, you may find that not only were the roots coming out of the drainage holes, but they are a solid mass inside the pot. If it is an older plant, there may not be much medium left, only roots.

Before repotting or up-potting, make sure your plant is well hydrated. A moist rootball is less likely to break apart when handled. If the pot is pliable, gently squeeze it to loosen the rootball, allowing it to come out of the pot. If it is a rigid container, cover the soil with your hand, turn the pot upside down, and it will usually slide out. If it doesn't, gently tug on the plant stem to see if it needs a small nudge to come out. If that fails, knock the pot on the side of a table and hopefully that will loosen the rootball. If all else fails, get a knife and run it around the rootball just inside the container wall. The last resort is to cut or break the pot.

Once the plant is removed, if the rootball is entangled and densely packed, it is important to tease the roots apart. If they are stuck to each other and difficult to pry apart, cutting the rootball becomes necessary. Most often, roots are a nice white color and should be firm. While you have the plant out of the pot, check for any unhealthy roots such as ones that are brown or mushy. Trim such roots off the plant. The desired result is to have a mass of roots that can spread out and grow. Slicing the rootball down the side at intervals all around stimulates the cut roots to send new roots out into the fresh potting medium. As you settle the plant into its new home, make sure room is left between the rim of the pot and the soil line. Small pots need ½ to 1 inch and large pots need 1½ to 2 inches or more. This allows you to water without the soil and water running over the side of the pot.

Large plants can become impossible to repot or up-pot. Yet, you can see the medium in these plants is decomposing. If you find that the roots are becoming visible in the container, it may be time to *top-dress* your plant. Simply add fresh medium to the top of the container to cover roots that are showing, making sure the medium is only covering the exposed roots, not the stem of the plant. Covering the stem with medium may cause problems, such as rot.

TIP: HAND PROTECTION

Wearing some type of gloves is a good idea while repotting or up-potting plants, especially if you have allergies or are working with sphagnum moss, which can cause a rash from the fungus sporotrichosis. (This fungus can also be contracted from working with roses and hay bales.) It is rare for this to happen, but wearing gloves will ensure there are no problems.

If you have a large plant that is the optimal size for your needs, you can keep it at that size for an extended length of time. If it were to get larger, you might have to discard the plant or give it away. There is a solution. You can trim the plant and, at the same time, prune the roots.

Remove your plant from the container and cut off the bottom third of the rootball. Scoop fresh potting medium in the container and replace the plant so that it is at the same level it was previously. Now, the top also needs to be pruned so that the pruned rootball can support the foliage that is remaining. Prune approximately the same length off the top of the plant as the depth of the roots removed. By doing this, you can keep your plant at approximately the same size for quite some time. It is better to do this on a regular basis than by trying to severely prune a plant when it has outgrown its allotted area.

The best time to up-pot a plant is when the plant actively starts to grow in the spring, when the days get longer and the plants start to send out new growth. The most conducive time begins in late February to early March and continues through the summer. Up-potting a plant in the fall or winter is not recommended, as houseplant growth slows down and almost ends during the short days and long nights.

Houseplant Containers

The container you choose for your houseplant is important. We've discussed the size of the pot you should put your plant in, but let's look at the types of pots there are to choose from.

You can choose from a never-ending array of containers to hold your houseplants.

The choices are endless. The materials are endless. The most common, though, are terracotta, plastic, and glazed terracotta or ceramic. These are the containers you will find at most garden centers, yet don't overlook less conventional vessels that will hold soil. A child's toy truck, elephant-shaped ceramic candle holder, and an antique McCoy pot can all make compelling containers.

The most common container is called a *standard-size pot*. This means the diameter at the top of the pot is the same as the height. You will also see *azalea pots*, which are three-quarters as tall as the diameter of the pot. Azalea pots are recommended for plants that don't have extensive root systems, such as begonias, cacti, and other succulents. A *bulb pan* is twice as wide as deep and is perfect for dish gardens. Choose a container that you like as well as one that is appropriate for your plant.

▶ This rooster planter was a vase, but with a drainage hole drilled in the bottom, it makes a perfect planter.

Do not use *bulbous pots* that are smaller at the top than the middle of the pot. These are sometimes called bean pots. Trying to get the plant out of a bulbous pot is almost an impossible task. The bulbous part of the soil and plant roots must be cut away to allow removal of the plant.

Bulbous pots are not recommended. They make it extremely hard to remove a plant from the pot as its opening is smaller than the middle.

Pebbles and plant pot shards are unnecessary additions to the bottom of a pot for drainage.

The only requirement of any container is proper drainage. This means a drainage hole, not gravel in the bottom of the pot. Using gravel or pebbles as drainage is unnecessary and not helpful. Studies have shown that water does not move easily from the small air spaces found in planting medium to the large air spaces surrounding gravel or shards. Using medium all the way to the bottom of the container will make a long column of planting medium, which gives the plant more room for roots. Covering the drainage hole with pot shards is also unnecessary. Instead, use window screening to cover the hole; the potting medium will stay in and the excess water will easily drain out.

Before planting, place a piece of screen over the hole to let water out but keep the potting medium in.

If you have a container without a drainage hole, it can be used as a *cachepot* (pronounced *cash-poe*), which is French for "flower-pot holder." Essentially, a cachepot is a decorative container used to hold a more utilitarian or unattractive pot inside. If I had a pot I didn't want to drill a hole in, such as an antique piece of pottery, I would go this route. Water the plant in the sink, allow the excess water to drain from the bottom of the planting pot, and return the plant to the cachepot. Or, if the plant is too large, water the plant in the cachepot and use a turkey baster to suck out any extra water in the bottom.

If, on the other hand, you want to drill a hole in a container, I suggest buying a masonry drill bit or a diamond-tipped drill bit. These bits, especially the diamond bit, make it a breeze to drill a hole in any vessel, even glass. Wear safety glasses and follow the directions provided with the bit.

Choose either a masonry bit or diamond-tipped drill bit to make a hole in your container.

This pot has the hole one-half drilled through the container using a ¼-inch diamond-tipped drill bit.

TIP: TAGGING HOUSEPLANTS

Plastic plant tags and a pencil to write on them are very helpful tools when repotting plants. Using permanent markers are fine for short-term tags, but for information to last on a plant tag, a pencil is best. Write the common name and botanical name of the plant, as well as the date it was repotted. You would be amazed how fast time goes by. You may find a plant seems to be struggling and when you look at the tag, the reason becomes clear when you see it has been more than five years since the plant has been repotted. You may also find it useful to record the place it was purchased, the price paid for the plant, and the date purchased.

The hole has been completely drilled through the container.

Potting Mediums

The *potting medium* you choose is important: The life of your houseplant depends on it. You can have the perfect window with the right amount of light and a healthy plant, but if the potting medium is not exceptional, your plant will decline rapidly. The medium sustains the plant by anchoring the roots in the container, supplying water and nutrients, and providing aeration. Therefore, the potting medium you use is crucial to the health of your plant. There are many potting medium choices, and many are specific to certain plant species. An all-purpose potting mix works well for most foliage plants, such as philodendron, pothos, and ivy. There are mixes specifically made for certain plant groups including African violets, cacti, and other succulents. African violet mixes are composed mostly of peat moss with perlite added for drainage. The cacti and succulent medium contains a fast-draining mix including sand and other components.

Choose a potting medium that is appropriate for the plant you are working with.

Potting mixes are sometimes referred to as *medium* or *media* instead of soil, as many mixes have no soil in them. Sphagnum peat moss is the main ingredient of most houseplant potting mixes. Because of concern about the mining of peat moss bogs, many companies have switched to coir, a byproduct of the coconut fiber industry. Both work well at holding water. Other ingredients added to potting mixes are vermiculite and perlite, which assist in drainage so the plant roots do not become waterlogged. Sponge rock is similar to perlite but the granules are larger; a common mix for epiphytic orchids is one part sponge rock to two parts chopped coconut husk fiber. A wetting agent is also used in peat-based mixes to assist with the rehydration of the peat. Often moisture-control beads and fertilizer are added to potting mixes. These mixes are more suited for outdoor containers.

Many potting mediums are too dense for houseplant root health. The roots cannot get enough air because the medium does not have enough aeration. Water cannot drain through the medium fast enough. Mixing approximately ⅓ part of a purchased potting soil, ⅓ part of vermiculite, and ⅓ part of perlite makes for a better-draining medium that is more conducive to the health of the plant.

No matter the medium you choose for your plant, make sure your container has drainage and that the health of your plant is considered. You may have to try a few mixes before you find the one that works with your watering practices and makes your houseplant thrive.

Watering and Fertilizing

Watering practices are the biggest killer of plants. Whether you tend to over- or under-water, watering can be the hardest thing to get right when taking care of a houseplant. Of course, the environment the plant is residing in makes a difference. The light the plant receives, the temperature of the home, and the humidity all play a part in the watering regime. A plant in bright light in a home kept at 75°F will need more water than a plant in low light and in a lower temperature. A sunny week will have a different effect on how much water is needed compared to a cloudy week. If a plant isn't receiving sun, it won't be photosynthesizing at its normal rate and so won't be using as much water. Also remember, your plants will need to be checked more often in the summer when the air conditioning comes on and in the fall when the heater comes on. Because the air conditioner and furnace both lower the humidity in your home, until your plants adjust, more water than normal may need to be added to the potting medium. Therefore, you can see why it isn't recommended to water your plants on a set schedule. Instead of watering every Friday, for example, checking your plants on a schedule is the best practice. Every plant you have does not need to be watered with the same amount of water or on the same day. The key is to check the plant to see if water is needed.

Inconsistency can play a huge part in the health of the plant. Letting your plant dry out too much and then drowning it is not beneficial. Keeping it consistently moist is a better practice.

Fertilizing plants is a practice that perplexes many and yet is beneficial to our plants. Because people are unsure how, or with what, to fertilize their houseplants, they often don't do it. There is nothing wrong with that if you have organic substance in your medium that is decomposing, thus providing your plants with nutrients. If, on the other hand, you are using a soilless mix, fertilizing is essential to the health of the plant. Soilless media have little nutritional value to the plants and so need to be supplemented with fertilizer. Remember the food plants need is generated by exposure to the sun or an electric grow light. Fertilizer is just an added bonus for your plants. Yet there are also growers who run for the fertilizer every time they perceive there is a problem with their plant. This can be detrimental to a plant. A sick plant never wants fertilizer, just like we don't want a full five-course meal when we aren't feeling well. Let's try to make these watering and fertilizing processes less mysterious and more beneficial to your houseplants.

Watering Your Plants

You can check your plant for its water needs in several ways. A *moisture meter* is an instrument that has a probe that is inserted into the soil. The attached meter registers a reading of wet or dry. Testing the dryness or wetness of a container can also be done by lifting the container. After you water your plant, lift the container to feel the weight. A week or so later, lift the container again. If it feels about the same, it doesn't need water. If, on the other hand, it is substantially lighter, it is time to water. Sometimes you can tell a plant needs water by the way it looks. This may be obvious by its color, as plants that are dry often turn a lighter green. This is especially true of ferns. A plant that has wilted also may be an indicator that the plant is dry. Make sure to check the potting medium, though, as it also may be an indication that the plant is too wet, the roots have rotted, and the plant can no longer take up water. Allowing a plant to dry out to the wilting point is detrimental to the plant and may be fatal. Needless to say, waiting until a plant wilts should not be used to determine when a plant needs water.

The best way to check your houseplant for moisture is to stick your finger into the potting medium. If it is moist at the first or second knuckle, put the watering can down. If it is dry, then give it a good drink.

This brings us to how much water to give your plant. Every plant has different water needs, but the technique is the same for all plants. Giving your plant just a little water, hoping you don't overwater your plant, is not the correct way to water. Water *every* plant until water runs out the bottom of the pot. This includes cacti and other succulents. The water draws air through the soil as it runs out the bottom, bringing air into the roots. Make sure to water all the way around the pot, not consistently in one spot every time. This ensures that the whole rootball is well moistened. Watering in the same spot every time can lead to root death in other spots in the pot that have dried out. Water moves down, not sideways. The key to this thorough watering practice is the amount of time that passes before you water again. It may be months before a cactus or other succulent needs water again, yet your fern or peace lily may need water again in a week. If you have a root-bound plant, it may need water again in a couple of days. The point is, every plant is different, and each one needs to be checked individually to see if it needs water. Never assume because one of your plants needs water that they all need water on the same day. In a perfect scenario, we could water all our plants on the same day with the same amount of water, but such perfectionism is not possible. Checking your plants and interacting with them makes for a better day anyway.

TIP: THE DRAINAGE HOLE

An integral part of successful plant watering is the planting container used, and the most important aspect of the container is the drainage hole. Every container used for growing plants needs a drainage hole. If the pot is valuable and drilling a hole is impossible, the container should be used as a cachepot, as discussed in Chapter 1. For less valuable pots without a drainage hole, a masonry or diamond-tipped drill bit can be used to drill a hole in almost any material.

Bottom watering is often used for African violets because cold water will leave marks on their leaves, as shown here.

Watering Practices

There are different ways to water your plants, and there are differing opinions about which way is best. There is no one correct way. Always do what works for the optimal health of your plants.

Top watering is the most common way people water their plants. Water the top of the soil, making sure you completely water all the way around the pot. Use enough water so that it runs out of the bottom of the pot and into the saucer. After 30 minutes or so, empty any water remaining in the saucer. Never leave a plant standing in water for an extended period, as it could lead to root rot. If your plant is too large to move off the saucer to empty water, a turkey baster can be implemented to draw out the excess water.

Bottom watering is quite often used to water plants that have been deemed inappropriate to water from the top. African violets are one example. Water is placed in the saucer under the pot and is drawn up into the soil. When the top of the soil is moist, you know the plant has received enough water and any excess water should be poured out. If bottom watering is used as the watering practice of choice, occasionally water must be flushed through the plant from the top to wash out any excess fertilizer salts from the rootball.

Wick watering is a way to water plants that involves filling a reservoir with water which is then drawn up to the plant through string. Acrylic string works better than cotton as it lasts longer; cotton products will rot more quickly. As long as the reservoir is full of water, the plant will remain moist. Usually this method of watering is used with a light potting medium so that the plant is not waterlogged. A very heavy soil is not appropriate for a wick-watering setup.

▲ The deli container used has two holes in the top: one for filling with water and the other for the wick to come out of.

▼ Dandy pots are a decorative wick watering system. The plant is potted directly into the top container.

A wick watering system allows one to relax a bit when it comes to watering, as the plant is continually watered by drawing water from a reservoir below the plant. One must keep only the reservoir filled.

Vacation Care

If you need to leave for a business trip or a vacation, plant care can become a challenge. A weekend trip shouldn't be a problem, unless you have bonsai, but an absence of more than a week may lead to the death of some plants if they aren't watered. Hopefully you have a friend or family member who will agree to take care of your plants. Make sure they don't think that "taking care" of them means watering them only the day you arrive home. Houseplants need to be checked at least weekly, if not more often. If you can get a fellow plant lover to watch your plants, they should thrive while you are gone. If you have a friend willing to do it, but who has no experience, write out detailed instructions for each plant. But if no one is available to help, there are a few things you can do to ensure you don't come home to a house full of dead or dying plants.

Make sure your plant is well watered before you leave. Also, check for any unwanted pests and deal with them before you go, so as not to come home to a large infestation.

Moving your plants away from the windows and turning down the heat will slow your plants' growth. If they aren't receiving as much light, photosynthetic processes will slow down and they will use less water. The cooler temperature will also slow the plant processes down.

If you have only a couple of plants, place them in a see-through dry cleaner bag to keep the humidity up. The water evaporating from the plant through its leaves will be slowed down, and the humidity that does escape will stay around the plant, keeping it hydrated.

Wick watering is also a choice while you are gone. A good technique is to add an acrylic wick (yarn, nylons, etc.) to your plant and run the wick to a container of water. The wick will pull the water to your plant as it is needed, keeping it moist as long as there is water available.

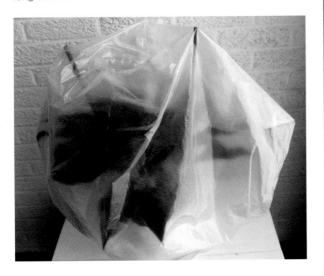

Self-watering pots have a glazed reservoir with the plant potted in an unglazed pot. The water seeps through the unglazed pot, watering the plant. These are often used for African violets.

Self-watering pots consist of two pieces of pottery. The bottom piece is glazed inside and out to retain water. The pot that sits inside the bottom pot is partially unglazed so that the water placed in the bottom pot can seep through the wall of the unglazed pot and keep the plant hydrated.

Immersion isn't commonly used as a watering practice, but it can be quite useful. It is most often used to rehydrate a plant that has been allowed to dry out. The potting medium may have shrunk away from the pot sides, allowing the water to run down the insides of the pot instead of soaking into the rootball. Standing the container in a basin of water, allowing the water to soak into the rootball and rehydrate it, works very well. Immersion also is used for tillandsias or air plants.

◀ If you have to be away from home, keeping your plants alive and watered can be a challenge. Place your plant in a large plastic bag to keep the humidity high and the plant from drying out.

Fertilizing Your Plants

Fertilizer comes in many forms and different formulas. The most important component to deciphering the fertilizer label is understanding the three numbers that appear on the container. What do they mean? The first number always represents the nitrogen (N) contained in the fertilizer, which keeps the plant green and promotes growth. The second number is phosphorous (P), which helps with root health and boosts flowering (it does not make plants flower). The third number is potassium (K), which boosts the plant's immune system, helping with heat and cold temperature tolerance and the overall health of the plant. There are also many micronutrients contained in fertilizer that help with the plant processes. These are usually present in any complete fertilizer.

There are two types of fertilizer to choose from: organic and nonorganic.

- Organic fertilizers build up the medium as well as give nutrition to the plant. There are many organic fertilizers to choose from, but a common one is fish fertilizer. After applying, there may be an odor for a time, but it is not too offensive. There are some types that aren't as odoriferous as others, so find one that works for you and the health of the plant.

- The nonorganic type of fertilizer is composed of artificial materials. The type most often used is the crystal-like form that normally turns the water blue. These are mixed with water and applied to the plant in your normal watering regime. Use a balanced fertilizer, such as 20-20-20 or 10-10-10 for all plants. If you possess a large number of one type of plant, you may want to buy a specialized formula made especially for that plant. For example, there is African violet fertilizer as well as orchid and cacti formulas. African violet and orchid food have high middle numbers to boost the flowering process of the plant. Cacti fertilizer has a lower amount of nitrogen, as it isn't as needed to promote green growth in these plants.

In general, a balanced formula works for most plants in your home.

Fertilizer comes in many forms; the water-soluble type is the most popular. Follow the directions on the label.

Fertilizer is available in many varieties. The form most often used by home gardeners is the water-soluble type. The crystals are measured into the watering can and water is added, making it an easy option since it is applied as the plant is watered. There is also fertilizer in liquid form, usually concentrated, which is added to your watering can. Another form of fertilizer comes concentrated in sticks. These are pushed into the soil evenly spaced around the pot, with the number of sticks used depending on the pot size. These tend to concentrate the fertilizer in small areas and may burn the roots, so sticks aren't recommended. The last type is a slow-release form of fertilizer. It is encapsulated in small ball shapes, and as the coating breaks down, it releases the fertilizer slowly in small amounts. This is recommended for outdoor containers, but as houseplants do not need fertilizer the entire year, this form is not the best. How often is fertilizer applied? How much is used? This is the only time you will be told to *not* follow the recommended application directions on the package. When it comes to fertilizing your houseplants, the "less is more" school of thought is the way to go. Since our plants are not growing in their optimum environments, they do not need a full-strength dose of fertilizer. Using your chosen type at ¼- to ⅛-strength every time you water is a better approach. That way your plant is receiving a continuous diet of added nutrients every time it is watered, rather than a heavy dose every month or so. That being said, remember that fertilizer is only given to houseplants when they are actively growing. Depending on your area of the country, this could be any time from February through late October. When the day length shortens in the fall, plants slow down their processes. When the days lengthen in late winter into early spring, our plants start sending out new growth. Because of these natural weather cycles, discontinue fertilizer in the late fall and start applying it again in the late winter into early spring, when the new growth is evident.

There is no doubt that watering and fertilizing your plants are important practices and ones that need a light, rather than heavy hand. Watch your plants and take your cues from them. If they look dry, they most likely are. If they look like they could use a boost of nutrients, they probably could. The key is to pay attention and check your plants on a regular basis. The signs are there, and if you are observant, you should have no problem keeping them well hydrated and nutrient-rich.

Propagation

There are many ways to propagate plants. Certain procedures work for some plants but not others. See the plant profiles in Chapter 5 for the best procedure for a particular plant.

The most popular way to make more plants is to take a *stem cutting*. Use a sharp knife or clippers to make sure you have a clean cut. Cut the stem ¼ to 1 inch below a node, cutting it at an angle. If you are taking a cutting of a succulent, allow the cutting to dry out for a few days and the end to callus over. Planting a cactus or other succulent cutting immediately after cutting may cause the cutting to rot.

Three stem cuttings from ivy, jewel orchid, and pothos plants.

Use a dowel or pencil to make a hole before sticking the cutting into the soil to ensure no damage is done to the end of the cutting.

Use a pencil or dowel to make a hole in the media to insert the cutting. Simply shoving the cutting into the media without making a hole first could damage the end of the cutting. Many different media can be used to root your cutting. Water, perlite, a perlite/vermiculite mix, or the potting medium usually used for your houseplants are all acceptable. Keeping the media moist is crucial for the cutting to root properly. Quite often, a covering is provided over the new cutting to raise the humidity. This can be done with a clear plastic bag over the container or by using a deli container with a clear top. It will take anywhere from 4 to 6 weeks for the cutting to form roots. If using water to start your cuttings, place them in potting medium soon after the roots start to form.

TIP: CUTTING AT AN ANGLE

When cutting your stems for propagation, cut your stem at an angle. If it is cut straight across, it has less area from which new roots can emerge. It doesn't have to be a perfect 45-degree angle; close enough is fine. The angled edge allows for more area to be in contact with the potting medium and to grow more roots.

TIP: CHIMERAS

Have you ever propagated a plant from a leaf cutting, only to have the resulting plant be a different color? It may be that you have tried to propagate a plant that is known as a *chimera*. These plants have patterns on the leaves or flowers that contain two or more colors distinctly separate from one another. A popular example of this type of plant is the 'Laurentii' cultivar of the snake plant, also known as mother-in-law's tongue. The plant leaf is banded with dark green, but also has yellow edges. Usually, the resulting "babies" born of leaf propagation will look exactly like their parent. If a chimera such as the 'Laurentii' is propagated from a single leaf, the beautiful yellow edge will not appear on the new plants. Instead, the only way to propagate the chimera snake plant is to separate a baby from the mother plant.

Leaf cuttings are another way plants are propagated. One leaf is all that is needed to make duplicate plants. Cut a leaf off, leaving at least a 1-inch petiole (the stalk that attaches the leaf to the stem). Insert the cutting into the potting media at a slant. If you are propagating an African violet leaf, in about 6 months, you will have a blooming-size violet all from one leaf! Rex begonias can also be started from one leaf. Cut slits across the veins of the leaf and lay the entire leaf on the surface of the potting media. Pin it to the media with florist pins or bent wire. The slit veins need to be in good contact with the media surface. The plantlets will grow where the veins were slit. Cuttings of the leaf with a section of the vein can also be used to start begonias. Other plants that can be started from a leaf section are snake plants, streptocarpus, peperomias, and many succulents, including echeveria.

If you have a dieffenbachia or anthurium that is leggy, you can take cuttings of the cane or stem and lay it horizontally on the media. Roots will form on the bottom, and the dormant nodes will grow. This method can be used for dracaenas as well.

A single leaf of many succulents can be simply placed on a pot of moist medium. They will eventually grow new plants.

If you have a plant that has more than one stem arising from the media, it can be *divided*. Remove the plant from its container, use a knife to slice through the roots, and separate the plants. If you do not want to use a knife, pry the plants apart, carefully teasing the roots apart. Pot them up in individual containers, watering them in well.

This *Aloe* 'Blizzard' has grown an offset, which can be separated and planted individually.

The parent plant and the smaller offset are cut apart with a knife.

The two plants have been separated and planted in appropriate size pots.

Some succulents in the Kalanchoe family produce small plantlets on their leaves.

Many plants provide miniature versions of themselves, ready to be separated from the parent plant. These are called *offsets*. Haworthias, agaves, and aloes all grow small plants at their base. They can be cut from the parent plant and rooted like any other cutting, or they may already have roots attached.

If you've ever seen a spider plant with all the little plantlets or spider babies swinging from the parent plant, you've seen a *runner* or *stolon*. These miniature versions of the parents swing from the plant in a hanging basket. You can cut a "baby" off and root it like any other cutting. A plantlet can also be pinned to a separate container of potting media and left attached to the parent plant until it forms roots. After it is well rooted, it can be cut from the parent plant. This allows the small plant to receive its water and nutrients from the parent plant while forming its own roots.

A close-up of the tiny plant complete with its own roots. It will drop off and grow on its own.

Tubers and Rhizomes

There are tuberous plants in the *Gesneriad* family such as gloxinias. These *tubers* can be divided by cutting them into pieces, each with a growing point, and potted up individually. Also in the *Gesneriad* family there are plants, such as kohleria, that are grown from scaly rhizomes that can be separated and planted individually.

Ferns that send out *rhizomes*, such as the rabbit's foot and bear's paw ferns, can be grown from pieces of those rhizomes that have a stem or frond attached. Cut these pieces from the main plant and pin them to a moist potting media until they root. Make sure the media stays moist while rooting takes place. It may be beneficial to cover the container with a plastic bag or glass dome to keep the humidity high while the plants are growing roots.

▶ The pregnant onion *Ornithogalum longibracteatum* grows small bulblets on its side that fall off, sprout, and grow new plants.

Many questions arise about what to do with an old, leggy plant. A favorite plant may hit the ceiling, and some might think the only thing to do is to throw the plant away, yet they do not want to lose a favorite plant. There is a solution called *air layering*. This process allows a plant to make a new set of roots while still attached to the parent plant, receiving water and nutrients. This process isn't a quick one, so patience is needed.

Choose the area where you would like the new roots to grow. If you would like to shorten your plant to 1 or 2 feet high, choose a spot that far from the top of the plant to work on. At that spot, use a knife to slice through the stem at an upward angle, only cutting approximately halfway through the stem. Place a toothpick or matchstick, depending on the size of the stem, in the cut to prop it open. Wrap damp sphagnum moss around that area and cover with plastic wrap.

Gather the supplies you will need to air layer your plant, including plastic wrap, a knife, a toothpick, moss, and twine.

Place a toothpick in the cut that has been made in the stem to hold it open.

Cut the toothpick so it doesn't put a hole in the plastic wrap that will surround the stem.

Wrap the cut area with damp sphagnum moss.

Encase the moss with plastic wrap.

Tie the top and bottom with twine, completely enclosing the moss in plastic wrap so it will stay damp.

▶ When completed, the cut area is enclosed with plastic, like a miniature greenhouse. When the roots fill the plastic wrap, it can be removed and the top of the leggy plant can be cut off and planted. The plant will be approximately 1 foot tall.

Be sure to secure the plastic carefully at the top and bottom. This creates a miniature greenhouse around the cut. In approximately 4 to 6 months, roots will grow into the moss. When the roots are obvious to you, the plant can then be cut from the parent plant and be potted up in an appropriate potting media. The remaining plant can then be discarded, or cut the stem lower and it may sprout a new plant from that cut point, giving you two plants.

Making new plants from old is a wonderful way to share plants with others. Plants make excellent gifts, and most people are thrilled to receive them. If you join a plant society, the members are very generous and more than happy to share their prize plants with others.

Grooming

We all need to *clean* our homes and the possessions in them. We mop floors, clean bathrooms and kitchens, wash windows, and the list goes on. Do you ever consider how dirty your plants become? Dust, pet fur, cooking grease, and more settle on the leaves, making their appearance shabby. Dirt and dust block the sunlight that gets to the plant and so cuts down on its photosynthetic process, which makes the food for the plant.

To keep your plants healthy and glowing, an occasional shower is called for. This does not have to be done weekly or even monthly; a few times a year is sufficient. Outside, our plants receive a shower every time it rains. If your plant is small enough to move, either give it a gentle spray in the kitchen sink or move it to the shower. Use lukewarm water, never too hot or cold, so as not to shock the plant. If your plant is too large to move, use a soft brush, cloth, or sponge to wipe the leaves clean. This is the time to mention that cleaning your plant's leaves only requires water and possibly a mild soap.

Do *not* use mayonnaise, milk, vegetable oil, or any plant-shine products. These are unnecessary and may even be detrimental to your plant. They can clog the stomates on the leaves, which are comparable to our pores. They allow dust to better adhere to the leaf and may even cause mold to grow or attract unwanted pests. Using milk may encourage your cat to chew the leaves.

All kitchen products are best saved for your favorite recipe—with one exception: use lemon or lime juice to remove white spots left on leaves by fertilizers, pesticides, or hard water. This is an especially pleasant way to groom the broad leaves of phalaenopsis (moth orchids).

Using lemon juice can remove residue left from hard water and fertilizers.

▶ Use pruners or scissors to trim the brown tip off the leaf.

▼ Browning may begin to spread further than the tips.

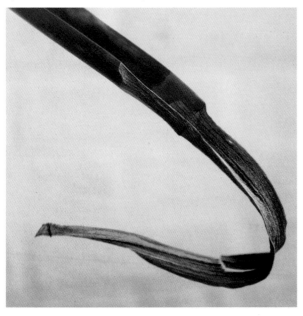

Pruning is something done to larger, woodier plants, such as ficus. These plants are often grown to tree size, and they may need to be pruned to keep them sized to the space. Bypass pruners will be needed for the thicker branches of these plants.

If a plant has outgrown its place in your home, more extensive pruning or cutting back may be needed. Up to one-third of your plant can be removed at one time; a reduction of the rootball may be beneficial at the same time. Try not to remove more than one-third in a single pruning, as this may kill the plant. Be cautious: try pinching and light pruning when the plant is young to keep it in check and avoid drastic pruning later.

The brown tip is gone, and the leaf is trimmed to the shape of the healthy leaves.

The *tools* for grooming your plants are easy to find and use. I use my bypass pruners for larger, woody plants such as a fiddle leaf fig. These woody stems can be hard to cut with small floral snips. Yet those snips are perfect for trimming small-leaved plants or topiary, which need precision. Scissors can work well to trim edges of leaves that have turned brown. Small, soft paintbrushes or a baby's hairbrush work well to gently brush off dust, especially from fuzzy leaves such as those found on the teddy bear plant (Kalanchoe). Don't underestimate the usefulness of your own fingers to pinch a plant when your scissors aren't on hand. Finding a branch of your favorite plant falling over the edge of the pot may require some bamboo stakes and twine to straighten it. Always use stakes and ties that blend in with the plant. Using brightly colored string and obvious stakes does not contribute to the beauty of the plant, and may detract from it.

Admittedly, pinching and pruning plants can be a daunting task to some. Keep in mind that *pruning* a plant is a natural process, one that happens in nature all the time. Keeping a plant's exuberant growth in check can make for a better-shaped, healthier plant.

It stimulates new growth and allows the plant to grow fuller. It is very important to remove any yellowing or brown leaves before disease moves in. If there is a leaf with a brown tip, trim just the tip, leaving the rest of the leaf intact. Do not cut the leaf straight across, though, but trim in the natural shape of the leaf, if possible. Always remember to wipe or dip your tools in alcohol to keep disease from spreading and insects being moved from plant to plant.

Pinching a plant is best done with the thumb and index finger. Pinching a plant involves removing a small amount of top growth to keep the plant full. Scissors, small pruners, and floral snips can also be used. Pinching works best when the plant is young and the growth is soft. Starting this practice early begins a training process that helps shape the plant. Letting a plant get out of shape with unchecked rampant growth may require drastic actions later. Keeping it in shape from the beginning is a better route to take.

TIP: SHARP AND CLEAN TOOLS

When grooming plants, it is important to make sure your tools are sharp and clean. Sharp tools ensure a clean cut is made when leaves or stems are removed. Ragged cuts encourage disease to enter the cutting, and dirty tools introduce disease to the cuts. Use rubbing alcohol to clean tools and ensure that your plants aren't introduced to anything that may harm them. This also prevents insects and disease being spread from one plant to another.

Brown leaf tips may be caused by many environmental factors.

3

Lighting

Placing your plant in the correct light situation is one of the most important factors of being a successful indoor gardener. Since plants make their own nutrients in conjunction with the sun, the source of light is of optimum importance. The act of taking light, water, and carbon dioxide and changing it into nutrition is called photosynthesis, a word many of us learned in school. Photosynthesis takes place only in the green part of a plant. The good news for humans and all other life on earth: oxygen is released as a by-product of the photosynthetic process.

Determining the amount of light a specific plant needs is not always easy, and you may experience a few casualties while figuring out the best situations for your plants. Light is measured in units called *foot candles*. Foot candles measure the amount of light visible to the human eye and are defined as the measure of light a candle casts on a surface one foot away. Humans see much less of the light spectrum than plants "see." We see the green-yellow part of the spectrum whereas plants use the red and blue parts. There are meters made to measure foot candles, but they are expensive and not necessary for a few houseplants. There is also a formula used to measure this with a camera. As most of the world uses smartphone cameras today, using a DSLR camera to measure the light for our plants is probably not feasible for most people. If you have a smartphone, there are apps you can download to let you know how many foot candles there are where you would like to place you plant. I'm not sure of their accuracy, so instead, let's talk about the window orientations in our homes and the plants they can support.

Sunlight

The four exposures in our homes have very specific types of light. It is extremely important to determine the orientation of your windows and whether they face east, west, north, or south.

If the sun comes up in the morning in your window, you have an *eastern exposure*. East light is a bright, warm light. It is not harsh and will not burn your plants. Ferns, begonias, prayer plants, aglaonemas, African violets, and many more do well in this exposure. This light is referred to as medium light. The light always comes in at an angle as the sun comes up and so the light penetrates far into the room, allowing for a larger amount of plants to be grown. Although plants further in the room will be exposed to medium light, the windowsill of an eastern window could be considered high light.

If the sun goes down in your window in the afternoon, you have a *western exposure*. Western light is also a bright light, but is consistently hotter than the east, as the afternoon light is harsher. This is also often considered a medium light, but may support quite a few high-light plants as well, such as succulents and cacti if they are close to the window. Because of the sun setting in this exposure, the sun also comes in at an angle as in the eastern exposure and allows a large number of plants to be grown further from the window.

Plants hung high in a window will receive less sun than those on a windowsill or ledge. Plants with more sensitivity to harsh light are best hung where they will not receive direct sun all day.

The *southern exposure* receives the most intense light throughout the day. If plants are placed on the windowsill or close to the window, it is considered high light and works well for cacti and other succulents, as well as other light-loving plants such as croton and ficus. Because the sun is high in the sky in the summer, the light shines down at a sharp angle close to the window. Plants placed higher in the window area will not receive as much sun as the area on the floor near the window. This means plants that need less sun can be placed higher or hung near the window. Because the sun is high in the sky in the summer months, the light in the southern exposure does not extend as far into the room as it does in

the east and west windows. It is a much stronger light, though. If plants are moved a few feet from a south window, or if there is a sheer curtain hung, a larger variety of plants can be placed in the southern exposure. As the sun is lower in the sky in the winter season, east and west window plants may be moved to the south window at that time so they receive better light. As the sun is lower in the sky in the winter, the light will go further into the room from the south during that season. It is also not as harsh as it is in the summer. The east and west exposures aren't affected as much by the seasons, as the sun comes in at an angle coming up and setting all through the year.

Northern exposure never receives any direct sunlight and therefore can support only low-light foliage plants such as the cast iron plant (aspidistra), philodendron, ZZ plant, and pothos. These plants are the ones usually found on the rain forest floor where they live happily in the shade with just dappled light. Blooming plants are not a consideration for the north window if you would like flowers unless you add supplemental light, which we will talk about later.

If you have a *skylight* in your home, you have a fifth exposure. The light will work its way across the floor as the sun moves across the sky, but will also add light to the whole room. If you have a bay window or a window that extends out from the side of the house, your plants will receive light from three exposures. If the window is on the north side, you have the added bonus of east and west exposure and that changes the light your plants are getting. Growing blooming plants has now become possible in a northern exposure. Garden windows are mini greenhouses, and growing a larger variety of plants is possible even if it is a small area.

TIP: VARIEGATED LEAVES AND LIGHT

If you've ever had a plant that had variegated leaves when purchased, but turned solid green after residing in your home for a time, you are not alone. This phenomenon is often encountered by houseplants that have come from the bright greenhouse into the lower-light situation in the average home. The solution is to move the plant to a brighter location or add supplemental light from an electric light source. After residing in a higher light situation for a few weeks, the variegation should return, if not to the old leaves, to the newly growing leaves.

Skylights and roof windows typically emit sunlight for most of the day, making them the spot for sun-loving plants or to pep up plants that have perhaps been languishing in dim conditions.

After evaluating the orientation of your window, there are other factors to consider. Obviously, the size of the window makes a difference. One must consider the presence of buildings, overhangs, trees, shrubs, and awnings. These all will greatly reduce the amount of sunshine coming into your window and falling on your plants. A south window may be considered a low-light area if a huge tree outside is casting shade on it. If it is a deciduous plant that drops its leaves in the fall, the light will greatly change and plants may be placed there until the leaves return in the spring. If there is a building next door, not too close in proximity, it may not impede the light at all. If it is a white or light-colored building, it may enhance the light falling in the window because of the reflection off the walls. Curtains or drapes will also change the amount of light allowed to fall on a plant. A sheer curtain in a south window may be a help to some plants as the light from a south window can be intense. If you want to grow medium-light plants in a south exposure, a sheer curtain would allow that.

Other factors to be considered, especially if your plants seem to be having problems, are the seasonal changes of light and weather changes from day to day. A week of cloudy days will change the water needs of your plants as will a week of very hot, sunny days. The longer days of spring and the shorter days of fall greatly affect the needs of your plants as well.

Enhancing the light you have can be done in a few different ways. The first way is to paint your walls a light color. A white or pastel wall will reflect the light and bounce it back to your plants. On the other hand, a dark wall will absorb the light, giving very little back to the plants. Another way to enhance the light in the area is with the use of a mirror. It reflects the light and benefits your plants at the same time. An easy, but often overlooked, way to enhance the light falling on your plants, is simply to clean the windows. It is amazing how dirty windows become, blocking light from entering. Rain, smog, and dirt in the air all can be deposited on windows throughout the year.

Window shades allow you to control light conditions as needed. If you are in an apartment with only western exposure, for example, shades will let you dim the harsh afternoon sunlight to prevent burning.

TIP: PHOTOTROPISM

Do you find that your plant is leaning toward the light? Or the stems have become stretched and do not look the same like the rest of the plant? This is called *phototropism* and is the growth of the plant toward the light source, whether a window or electric light. It is caused by the *auxins* (a type of plant hormone involved in growth) moving to the dark side of the plant and causing quicker growth on the dark side, thus bending the shoot toward the light source. The solution is to turn the plant regularly to keep the plant from having to bend toward the light, as it will be receiving light equally on all sides. If phototropism occurs unchecked for too long, or is happening to a plant with a woodier stem, turning the plant may solve the problem in the future, but the stem will be left with a permanent crook or bend. When the plant is young, regularly and faithfully rotate it to prevent any permanent scars.

Mirrors and white walls can help plants in otherwise dim conditions by reflecting what little light there is. This *Epipremnum aureum* is doing well in a bathroom without any window exposure at all.

Washing windows is especially important in the fall when the length of the days is shortening and many are bringing plants in from their summer vacations outside. Plants need all the light they can get to help them adjust from moving from the bright light they have been in outside. Screens cut down on the light coming through your windows, so make sure they are clean as well.

What are some indicators that your plant is receiving too little light? Usually, the first indicator is the leaning into the light. The new growth may also be pale with small leaves, plants may stretch and lose their shape. Many people wonder why normally blooming plants, such as African violets, do not bloom. The answer is, more often than not, insufficient light is falling on the plants. Root rot can also be an indicator of too little light, as the plant cannot use all the water it has been given, which will lead to mushy roots. This can occur even if the plant is not left sitting in water, which is usually the reason plants rot.

On the other hand, plants can let you know that they are receiving too much light. Too much light can also mean too much heat for plants, and they will usually indicate that by wilting. Hopefully you can move them away from the window a short distance and that will rectify the problem of excessive heat and light. Another plant reaction is to curl its leaves down toward the container, trying to get away from the light. This is obvious on African violets that are receiving too much light. The growth can also become compact and stunted from excessive light. Plants can also get sunburned. This can happen when a plant has been moved to a high-light area from a low-light area. If you feel your plant is getting too little light, move it gradually into the brighter light, giving it time to acclimate to the higher light. Move your plant to a shadier location, add an awning to your window, or perhaps plant a deciduous tree or shrub where it will cast some shade on your window from the exterior.

If these problems are ignored for too long, too little or too much light can eventually stunt a plant so severely that it may not recover and death may follow. Watch your plants closely and listen to what they are telling you.

Electric Light

Electric light makes it possible to grow plants without a window in the vicinity or to grow more plants when the windowsill space runs out. Many who grow African violets embrace the idea of electric lights as it allows them to have blooming plants all year long with more symmetrical growth. It also allows growers of cacti and other succulents in the northern areas of the country to grow their plants without the legginess they experience in the low-light levels in the winter.

There are three aspects of electric light: quality, duration, and intensity.

- The *quality* of light refers to the color of the light. Light is made up of the colors of the rainbow, as we see when it passes through a prism. The colors plants use, though, are red and blue. The red light allows the plant to form flowers, and the blue light helps the foliage grow and stay compact.

- The *duration* is the length of time a plant gets light in the day. Of course, at the equator, daylight and dark are equal every day of the year, 12 hours of light and 12 hours of dark. In the Northern hemisphere, the length of the day depends on the time of year.

- The *intensity* of the light refers to the amount of light a plant receives. This is where the bright light, medium light, and low light scale comes in. It is hard for our human eyes to determine this, but your plants will let you know quite soon if they are not happy with the intensity of light they are receiving.

Photoperiodism is the reaction plants have to the length of days and nights. Short-day plants need short days and long nights to bloom. These include poinsettias, holiday cactus, and kalanchoes. They need uninterrupted dark nights for at least 12 hours. Long-day plants need long days and short nights to bloom. These include most of our outside annuals.

Day-neutral plants do not need a short day or long day to grow well or flower. The equal hours of light and dark suit these plants. Day-neutral plants include African violets and other Gesneriads.

Types of Electric Light

There are many types of electric light, but only a few are suitable for houseplants.

The most common type of light and the one familiar to most people is *incandescent light*. These are the light bulbs we usually use in our lamps to read by and light our homes with. Unfortunately for the person growing plants, incandescent light is very hot and can't be placed close to the plants for fear of burning them. Incandescent lights only emit the red waves of light which encourages blooms, but isn't so great for the foliage. Sometimes incandescent is used in conjunction with fluorescent lights.

Fluorescent lights are the most common fixtures used with houseplants. They run cooler than incandescent bulbs and have a broader spectrum of light. Fluorescent lights come in many sizes. Two- and four-foot sizes are the easiest for the homeowner to handle.

Using a cool white bulb paired with a warm white bulb covers both the blue and red spectrum needed for flowering and foliage health. There are also daylight and full-spectrum bulbs that have everything a plant needs in one bulb. Pair one of those bulbs in the light fixture with a regular fluorescent bulb as the specialty bulbs are much more expensive.

In the past, the only size available was the T-12 bulb, which is the bulb seen in offices, workshops, and commercial buildings. The T stands for the diameter of the bulb measured in ⅛-inch increments. Recently T-8 and T-5 bulbs appeared on the market. The T-12 bulbs are 1.5-inch diameter, the T-8 bulbs are 1-inch diameter, and the T-5 bulbs are 0.62-inch diameter. With these long bulbs, the most light is given off in the middle of the bulb with the least light coming from the end areas. As the lights age, their light output decreases. The narrower the bulb is, the more efficient the light is. The T-5 and T-8 are becoming popular as they last longer and their light output loss is much slower than the T-12 lights. The smaller lights last almost twice as long as the larger lights. Because they are a lower wattage, they take less energy to run and because of their higher intensity light, they do not have to stay on as long. The T-12 lights are usually kept on for at least 12 hours per day, whereas, the T-8 lights are only on approximately 8 hours per day. They may cost more at first, but are worth it in the long haul. The cost is coming down, as well, as they become more popular.

Fluorescent lights do need to be quite close to the plants, though, which may not be ideal if you want to grow taller plants. Plants grown under lights have to be approximately the same size. For flowering plants, the lights are usually placed 6 to 12 inches above the plants and for foliage plants, 12 to 24 inches.

LED lights are the newest lights for the indoor gardener. How do they compare to fluorescent lights? They are more efficient, and though they cost more in the beginning, they will be more cost effective in the long run. The lights come in red and blue, which unfortunately turn your light growing area pink. It is good for your plants, but many do not like how the pink color makes the plants appear. If you are growing your plants to enjoy their flowers and foliage, the distorted color of your plants may not be acceptable.

Fortunately, LED lights are also becoming more available in white, allowing plants to receive both color waves they need. LED lights can be placed farther away from the plants, so taller plants can be grown under the lights.

I'm only going to mention metal halide, mercury discharge, and low and high pressure sodium lights briefly as there really aren't many houseplant growers using them. They are very large and emit a lot of heat. These are usually used for lighting a very large area and are quite often used in commercial situations or for cannabis production. If you have a large number of plants in a large area, these may be useful.

When using artificial light, make sure a reflector is used which will guide the light downward to the plants. Also, make sure the lights and fixtures are dusted on a regular basis. Any accumulated dust on the light fixtures lowers the amount of light getting to the plants. If you are using fluorescent lights, they need to be changed yearly as they start losing their light intensity with age. The ends of the tubes eventually turn black and need to be changed at that time. It is a good idea to write the installation date on the ends of the bulbs with a grease pen so that it is easy to remember when they should be changed. An important item in a light garden is a timer. Your plants will receive the same light every day on a regular basis without you having to remember to turn them on and off.

Whether you choose to only use the sunlight in your home garden or supplement with electric light, most importantly, watch your plants for their reactions. Move plants around if need be until they seem happy in the light they are receiving.

Newer LED lights can be much smaller than the fluorescent shop light fixtures we are familiar with. They are much more cost efficient to use as well.

4

Problem Solving

When growing houseplants, you eventually run into a problem or two. The best way to ward off potential complications is to buy healthy plants. Inspect your purchase before bringing it into your home. When you are at the garden center, scrutinize the plant closely. Not only look at the top of the plant, but turn the leaves over to look underneath. Pests love to hide under the leaves, but also in the leaf axils, where the leaf meets the stem of the plant. It is more difficult to control pests when they hide in tight places.

When you have picked out your plant at the garden center, always make certain it is wrapped up before leaving. It depends on the type of plant, but this is important if the temperature is below 50°F for most tropical plants. A paper wrap, not plastic, is best for protecting plants. Wrapping protects them not only from low temperatures, but also from windy conditions. If you have other errands to run, do not leave your plant in a cold or hot car. Either extreme temperature can harm a plant very quickly. Buy your plant and head home to unpack it.

Upon arriving home, find a room in which to quarantine your plant. It should be isolated for at least a month. This gives undetected pests time to make their appearance. If your plant is quarantined, it is less likely your other houseplants will be infected if there is a problem. If, after the month, the plant is pest- and disease-free, it can safely be placed among your other houseplants.

Keeping your plants well-hydrated, clean, and taken care of goes a long way in preventing pests and diseases. A healthy plant is less likely to contract problems than a plant that is under stress. This is a good time to remind you to inspect your plant closely every time you water. Turn your plant and at the same time pay attention to any obvious problems, such as yellowing or dropping leaves, distorted growth, or wilting.

Pests

Once you realize your plant may be having a problem, such as slow or distorted growth, the next step is to find and identify what is causing the problem. Is it an insect or a disease? Let's start with the obvious: pests.

Start by examining the top and bottom of the leaves, including the leaf axils. Bugs like to hide from sight and eat in peace and quiet, undetected for as long as possible. A magnifying glass or jeweler's loupe is a big help, especially if your eyesight isn't as sharp as it used to be. Let's talk about what to look for.

The first indicator that there may be a problem is the presence of a shiny, sticky substance on the leaves, container, or even the floor. This substance is called honeydew: it's the excretion from insects that are sucking the juice out of the plant. If you detect this, you can be sure there is a problem that needs to be addressed. If the problem is advanced, there may be a black substance accompanying the honeydew. This

is black sooty mold; it grows on the honeydew. The mold may be more obvious to the naked eye than the shiny honeydew. This sticky insect excretion is also attractive to ants. So the presence of ants may also be an indication there is a problem with your plant. Ants can move the insects from plant to plant and may take up residence in the plant's root zone. Most likely, ridding the plant of the pest creating the honeydew will take care of the ant problem as well. There are several common houseplant pests.

Foliar mealybugs are obvious to the naked eye, unlike some pests. If you detect a white fuzzy substance on your plant, especially in the axils of the leaves, you may be witnessing a foliar mealybug infestation. They appear as small tufts of cotton stuck to your plant. The white substance is protecting the small, slow-moving scale.

Foliar mealybugs are the houseplant owner's nightmare. They take up residence in any nook or cranny they can find on a houseplant. They settle in, get comfortable, and suck the life out of your plant. They are hard to eradicate, but with consistency, they can be brought under control. If they are detected early in the game, they are easier to deal with. Dip a cotton swab in rubbing alcohol and touch each cottony area. The alcohol will desiccate and kill the insect. Follow up with a spray of Neem oil or horticultural oil to smother any missed insects. Insecticidal soap may also be used to help control the infestation. Foliar insecticides may be sprayed on the plant in a well-ventilated area or outside. A systemic insecticide may be needed if the infestation is severe. This chemical is applied to the potting medium and is taken up into the plant. When the insect sucks the juice of the plant, it is poisonous, and the insect dies. Find what works best for you and your plant. Whatever route you choose to take, always read the entire label on any product you plan to use and follow the instructions to the letter.

Mealybugs are slow-moving scale that use their mouthparts to suck the juices from the plant leaves and stems.

It may be hard to detect just one mealybug, so look closely at your plants often.

Touch each mealybug or scale with rubbing alcohol on a cotton swab.

Root mealybugs hide in the potting medium. If the plant is deteriorating and there are no visible signs of a problem above, take the plant out of the pot and examine the roots.

Root mealybugs are more difficult to detect. They resemble pieces of rice stuck to the roots of plants. They aren't obvious as they are out of sight in the potting medium, but indicators are slow growth and wilting leaves. If no other insects are evident, take the plant out of its container and examine the roots. They also excrete honeydew, which may present itself as sticky spots on the inside of the pot. These insects can spread through water among plants sharing the same saucer. They can also spread through the potting medium.

If your potting medium is stored in a large container that you also use to repot or up-pot your plants in, you could be spreading the bugs to your other plants. Do not repot your plants in or near your planting medium storage container. If you find you have these insects, rinse all the old medium off your roots and repot in fresh medium. Use a clean new pot, or disinfect your old container before placing your plant back into it. A systemic insecticide in the medium will also help get any mealybugs or eggs that are still lurking.

You will usually find aphids on the new growth of plants; they may be red, green, yellow, or black.

Scale are brown oval spots that attach themselves to the plant and suck out the juices. Black sooty mold forms on the honeydew they secrete.

Aphids, also called plant lice, are almost always found on the new growth of a plant. They can be detected by the naked eye, as they may be black, red, yellow, or green. Rather than laying eggs, mother aphids have live births and so multiply rapidly. They secrete honeydew, which can grow sooty mold. Leaves can curl under and become deformed by the aphids. Unfortunately, aphids can also carry viruses that they may transmit from plant to plant. The easiest way to rid your plant of aphids is to spray them with a strong stream of water, which knocks them off. A contact insecticide or systemic may also be used. Do not use fertilizer with a high first number, which promotes fast growth. This new, tender growth is like a dinner bell for the aphids.

Scale insects are like mealybugs, but instead of a fuzzy white covering, they have a light brown covering that blends in with the plant. The adults do not move, but young nymphs, unable to be seen by the naked eye, move around until they find a place to settle down. Scale can attack almost any plant; they also secrete a sticky honeydew. This may be the only visible indicator. Scale is often hard to see and may look like a part of the plant.

Scale insects are difficult to control with an insecticide, as they have a hard covering that protects the insect underneath. If there are only a few present, picking them off by hand is effective, as is scraping them off with a stiff toothbrush. If they are many of them, a systemic insecticide may be your best course of action. Neem oil or horticultural oil may work to cover and suffocate them. Again, read the label to be certain the chemical you are using can be applied to your plant. Many chemicals cannot be used on ferns, for example.

Thrips are extremely small and almost undetectable to the human eye. A good indicator, at least on flowering plants such as African violets, is the presence of pollen on the petals. The thrips like to eat the pollen sacs, which spills pollen onto the flowers. They have rasping mouth parts and scrape the leaves as well, which gives them a silvery appearance. If you suspect thrips are present, breathe on the plant and, if you have good eyesight, you will see them scurry for cover. Removing the flowers will help control the populations of thrips on your plants. Spray the plant with an insecticide that lists thrips as an insect it can control. Repeated sprays will be necessary as they like to hide deep in the flowers and plants, and they may be missed the first time.

There are a couple of types of mites that may be encountered in the home. The first is the *spider mite*. Spider mites seem to attack mostly dry plants. They are exceptionally busy in the cold months when the heaters are going full blast. The air is dry, and the spider mites appear for the feast. They are hard to see and may be present in large numbers before they are detected. If you suspect an attack of spider mites, shake a leaf over a piece of white paper. If dark specks fall and begin to move, spider mites are present. If left untreated, the webbing they create will become obvious to the naked eye and small mites might also be seen. They are not insects, though, but in the arachnid family with spiders. To prevent them, keep your plants well hydrated and place them on a pebble tray to keep the humidity high around the plant. If you find that your plant has mites, start by washing them off and then use a mite killer, as an insecticide will not work on them. Neem oil or horticultural oil could also be used.

Cyclamen mites are bugs that are almost impossible to see. And while they may infest cyclamen, they are more likely to be detected on an African violet. The flower centers will become deformed and very tight and fuzzy. If this happens to your violet, it is best to throw it away immediately before it spreads to your other plants. Use a miticide that is labeled for use on cyclamen mites. Neem oil may also be effective.

If you've ever noticed small black flies occasionally flitting around your home, you may have *fungus gnats*. Many people assume they are fruit flies, but if you have no overly ripe fruit, yet have plants, chances are they are fungus gnats. These insects live in the top few inches of your moist potting medium. The larvae live in the medium, eating organic matter and roots. The adult flies are more a nuisance and an indicator that the larvae are present in the medium. To control them, remove any plant debris that is in the container as they will feed on it. Fungus gnats are attracted to and live in potting medium that is left moist at all times. Because they live in the top few inches of the medium, let it dry down 2 to 3 inches before watering again. If the infestation has been abundant, remove the top couple of inches of potting medium and replace it with fresh. If they seem quite abundant, a systemic insecticide can be applied to the potting medium. Yellow sticky traps may be used in plants to monitor the numbers of insects present.

Whiteflies are just what they sound like—small white flies that arise from the foliage if at all disturbed.

Whiteflies are not flies at all, but are more closely related to aphids and scale. These insects are usually found on the underside of leaves where they feed on the juices of the leaves. There they lay eggs, raise their young, and feed on the plants. When the plant is disturbed, the whiteflies fly up in your face. Using yellow sticky traps will monitor the numbers of the insects. They will secrete honeydew, another indicator of their presence on your plants. Ridding plants of whiteflies is not always successful. Try using Neem oil or horticultural oil to suffocate the young. Insecticidal soap may also work, as well as a systemic insecticide used in the soil. Since they fly, vacuuming them up will be effective in removing the adults.

TIP: QUARANTINE YOUR PLANT IF YOU SUSPECT A PROBLEM

If you have a feeling that something is amiss with your plant, the first thing to do is remove the plant from the vicinity of other plants. Check the plant thoroughly for disease or insects to detect the problem. If something is found, treat it appropriately and keep it quarantined from your other plants until you are sure the problem has been dealt with successfully. Keep an eye on surrounding plants for the appearance of the same problem.

Diseases

Occasionally, the problems with our plants have nothing to do with insects, but may be a disease. These can be caused by many things, but can be solved by changing your growing and care practices. If the disease or damage is advanced, throwing a plant away may be the best course of action to prevent it spreading to nearby plants. The issue may stem from environmental issues such as cold damage or sunburn. These things are usually easy to rectify. But what else should you be looking for?

Powdery mildew presents itself as a white powdery substance on the leaves or sometimes on the stems of plants. These are fungal spores and are spread by water or a breeze. The plants most often attacked are African violets, begonias, and ivy. Poor air circulation combined with low light and cool temperatures are the factors that contribute to the growth of this fungus. If it is left untreated, it can spread to all parts of the plant and eventually may kill it. By keeping your growing area well-ventilated, spreading your plants apart so they are not crowded, and keeping the leaves dry, powdery mildew shouldn't be a problem. If it does appear, removing the affected parts of the plant is one solution. Spraying your plant with a fungicide is another, but should be done outside. Neem oil also works well.

This Norfolk pine was left against a freezing cold window all winter, which killed the tips of the branches. This could happen with a hot window in the summer as well. Avoid allowing your plants to touch the windows.

Crown rot usually is not apparent until your plant keels over. It occurs when potting media has been kept too wet. This coupled with high humidity, poor ventilation, and too high or too low temperatures sets your plant up for crown rot. If you catch the problem before the plant completely collapses, take cuttings from the healthy parts of the plant to ensure you don't lose it completely. To prevent crown rot, pay attention to the soil moisture and temperatures around your plants, and use a good potting medium that is light and drains quickly. Another factor that could induce crown rot is planting your plant too deeply in the medium when repotting. Buried stems are sure to rot.

It is perplexing when a leaf develops a brown or yellow spot and for no apparent reason. But if water is left on the leaf too long, this may cause *leaf spots*. They may be viral or bacterial, and it may be hard to diagnose. If it is on the edge of the leaf, the spot may be trimmed off. If it spreads, the entire leaf should be removed. A fungicide or Neem oil may help as well. To prevent leaf spot, do not allow water to sit on the leaves of the plant for an extended length of time and increase air movement to prevent stagnant air.

Black sooty mold grows on the honeydew secreted by certain insects. It is an indicator of a bigger problem, which is the pest that is causing the accumulation of honeydew. Getting the insect or mite problem under control is the first order of business. Wipe down or shower your plants to remove the mold and honeydew. Keep a closer eye on your plants to discover an insect problem quickly before the honeydew and mold occur.

This spot beginning on the aglaonema leaf is a fungal disease. To prevent the disease from spreading, the leaf should be removed, or it should be sprayed with a fungicide.

This leaf was burned by the sun because water sat in its indentation. Be careful when placing a plant back in a sunny spot after overhead watering or cleaning.

Environmental Damage

Houseplants may have problems that aren't caused by pests or diseases, but by the environment they are living in or the way they are cared for. These problems can arise from being too hot or too cold, the water being used, fertilizer damage, and more. They can be rectified easily by paying closer attention to the situation the plant is in and the practices used to care for them. The key to successfully helping your plant is to determine the cause of the problem before changing the environment, possibly causing more damage.

It may be hard to believe that a plant can become *sunburned* just as we do. Most often this happens when plants are taken outdoors for the summer or placed in a bright sunny window. It may be a cactus or other succulent or a plant that is known to love a sunny window. How could it sunburn? While these plants may be able to handle these high-light situations, the problem occurs when they are taken from a low-light situation, such as a home, and placed in a high-light situation. Instead, the plant needs to be slowly moved to the higher-light situation by first placing it in a slightly higher-light situation and then, after a few weeks, if the plant is able to withstand the increased light, it will be fine in its new situation. The same thing can happen inside: gradually move the plant to higher-light situations until it is in its final position.

Cold damage to plants doesn't necessarily mean the temperatures are below freezing. Houseplants may be damaged at temperatures below 50°F, but usually damage doesn't present itself until temperatures are in the low 40s and into the 30s. Whereas some plants are fine with these lower temperatures, many of our tropical plants drop leaves and may even die. Houseplants do best at temperatures between 60 and 80°F, with a slight drop in temperatures at night. If you are comfortable, most likely your plants are too.

Some plants are more susceptible to *browning leaf tips* than others. Plants such as the spider plant, prayer plant, and dracaenas are very sensitive to dry air, fertilizer salt buildup, and damage caused by inconsistent watering practices. Trim the tips, mimicking the shape of the other leaves, and adjust the care factors contributing to the brown tips.

Fertilizing is good for your plants if done in the correct manner. If plants are watered from the bottom as a rule, *salt burn* can damage your plants. The salts from the fertilizer can build up and not only cause damage to the tips of your plant leaves, but can cause damage to the roots and hinder the uptake of water into the plant. The weakened plant can then be a target for pests and diseases. The solution is to run water through the plant from the top until it runs out the bottom. This flushes excess salt from the plant and prevents buildup. It may be time to repot your plant using fresh potting medium as well. The salt can build up on the edges of containers and is especially apparent on clay pots as a white crust. Before repotting with fresh medium, scrub the buildup off the pots. Soaking your pots in vinegar is helpful in dissolving the crust and making it easier to scrub it off. Make sure all the vinegar is washed off the container before placing a plant into the pot.

Plants may *wilt* for a few different reasons. The first and the most common reason is that the plant needs water. Yet sometimes a plant wilts because it has root rot from overwatering. It may also be from crown rot,

which will cause the plant to wilt and collapse. The first thing to do is determine the reason for wilting and hopefully rectify the problem.

An occasional *leaf dropping* off a plant is a common occurrence and should not be a cause for worry. If, on the other hand, the floor is littered with leaves, there is most likely a problem. Quite often, if a plant is moved from a high-light situation to low light, the plant reacts by dropping leaves. If there is insufficient light to support all the leaves, it will drop as many as it needs to. This often happens when plants are moved inside in the fall, after being outside for the summer. They need to be slowly acclimated to lower light just as they were going outside into higher light. This needs to be a gradual process. Plants may also drop leaves if they have been over- or under-watered. If it has been overwatered and the roots are dying, leaves will drop from lack of water. If the plant is under-watered, the leaves will drop from the same problem. Consistent, even moisture is best for a plant. Plants may also drop leaves from being too cold or hot, or from insects or disease. Inspect your plant to ascertain what the problem is.

Nothing is more exciting than seeing flower buds appearing on your plant. You wait patiently in anticipation of a flower display. Then the buds fail to open and fall off or dry up. How disappointing! *Flower bud drop* may signal that the plant was allowed to dry out too much at a critical time. If the humidity is too low, the buds may not fall off but fail to open. Some plants are sensitive to being moved too much or at all after they have set their buds. Keep your plant evenly moist while flowering, and keep the humidity up around the plant. This can be done with a humidifier or by use of a pebble tray.

If your plants display *leaves that are a color different than the other leaves*, it may only be the new growth. Often, new leaves are a lighter green when they first unfurl: that is nothing to be alarmed over. They will eventually turn the same color as the older leaves. If, on the other hand, they remain off-color, or the veins are green and the leaves are yellow or the other way around, they may be experiencing a nutrient deficiency. This may be an indicator that the pH of the planting medium is not in the optimum range for the plant. If the pH of the medium your plants are growing in is too high or too low, nutrients cannot be released to the plant. This will present itself quite often with off-color leaves. Use a pH meter to test the level in your media and change it if needed. Most plants are fine around 6.0 to 6.5, but if it is much higher or lower, it may be harming the plant. Yet there are some plants that prefer an acid (4.0 to 7.0) or an alkaline (7.0 to 9.0) soil. If a problem is detected, repotting the plant in a fresh medium may help.

Taking good care of your houseplants and keeping them healthy goes a long way toward keeping complications to a minimum. The healthier a plant is, the less likely it is to be attacked by pests and diseases. Keep the growing area clean, pick up any dead leaves and flowers, and make sure the potting medium is well-drained and fresh. Keep your tools and hands clean. That is very important if you are working on more than one plant, as you may spread things from one plant to another. Don't come in from working in your outside garden and work on your indoor plants. Insects and disease spores may hitch a ride inside on your clothes or even your hair.

Enjoy working with your plants and pay close attention as you water and groom them to catch any issues that may occur before they become catastrophes.

Yellowing leaves can be an indicator of under-watering, overwatering, too high temperatures, too low temperatures, and more. More investigation will be needed to ascertain the problem.

Plant Profiles

In this section, we will cover the care of individual houseplants. They are broken into three groups: easy to grow, moderately easy to grow, and challenging to grow. The houseplants considered challenging may not necessarily be that much harder to grow than an easy or moderately easy plant, but just need more attention. If you don't have the time and want to make sure your plant thrives without too much effort, choose a plant from the easy to grow section. If you like a challenge and have the time and inclination, try one in the challenging section. Of course, everyone's growing conditions are different and you may find that a plant in the challenging section is super easy for you to grow. These are categorized as to how I have found them to grow in my experience and growing conditions.

No matter which one or more you share your home with, hopefully they thrive and make you happy—which is all that really matters anyway. Remember, killing a plant is only a learning experience and shouldn't discourage you from trying again. There is a plant out there for every home and growing condition. Happy growing!

EASY TO GROW

These plants will make anyone feel as if they have a green thumb. These plants are without complicated care and are forgiving of care that isn't always right on point. Pick one or more of these plants and enjoy nurturing a plant of your own.

AIR PLANT

BOTANICAL NAME: *TILLANDSIA*

In their native habitats, air plants grow on trees and are epiphytes, which are plants that grow on other plants, but are not parasitic. They only use them for a place to rest and take nothing from the host plant. They are easy, versatile plants that have taken the houseplant world by storm. The ease of care, accessible cost, and versatility make this a plant for everyone. Though these plants are commonly called air plants, they do need water to live. They naturally live in places with high humidity and so need less actual water, but in our heated, low-humidity homes, they will definitely need to be watered—in their case, soaked—on a regular basis.

LIGHT PREFERENCE: Air plants need a bright light to do their best. An east or west window works and some may appreciate a south window. If light is at appropriate levels, they will flower and send out babies.

WATERING: Soak air plants once a week in tepid water for approximately 30 minutes, drain upside down for a short time and return them to their growing area. Some recommend distilled water, but tap water works as long as its chemical content isn't high. These plants naturally grow on an angle, so water never sits in the middle of the plant. If it does, the plant may rot and fall apart. Like any plant, the more light they receive, the more water they will use. They love humid air, so a home in the kitchen or bathroom is perfect, if there is enough light.

FLOWER: The small flowers are brightly colored, often with purple flowers, and protrude from colorful bracts.

SIZE: This large family of plants range in size from under 1 inch to 3 feet and more.

PROPAGATION: As the plants grow and mature, they will send out offsets—"babies" or "pups"—from their base. When these new plants are approximately one-third the size of the parent, they can be removed. If preferred, they can be left on the parent plant, and a large clump of plants will form.

CULTIVARS: There are many varieties of air plants out there, and many are easy to grow in the house.

- *TILLANDSIA IONANTHA*—The most common air plant sold to the consumer, it may reach 2 to 3 inches tall and sends out plenty of offsets at its base with enough light and appropriate water.

- *T. USNEOIDES*—Dripping from trees in the south, Spanish moss is an icon of that region. Many people don't even realize it is a living plant. Maybe that comes from the fact that dried Spanish moss is sold in craft stores for projects. It needs to be soaked the same as the other tillandsias and hung to dry. It is a light green/gray color when living and turns brown when dead.

- *T. XEROGRAPHICA*—The Greek word *xeros* means to dry. These large plants naturally grow in dry forests of Mexico and enjoy full sun. These need less water and more sun than other tillandsias, so be careful not to overwater and rot them. If in intense light, they will need more water than if in a medium light. They may not need to be soaked weekly like the other members of the family.

- *T. TECTORUM*—This fuzzy-looking tillandsia can be grown in high light and actually prefers it. The fuzzy silver covering helps protect it from the sun in its native habitat. It loves extremely high humidity to go along with the high light. This is a very striking plant.

ALOE VERA

BOTANICAL NAME: *ALOE VERA (ALOE BARBADENSIS* syn.)

The medicinal properties of **ALOE VERA** are touted extensively and for good reason. Have you ever burnt your finger and found the amazing relief that using aloe gave you? It also soothes and cools a sunburn. The great thing is that you can grow your own! This is a succulent that is easy to grow in bright light, and it sends out many offsets, making it easy to share with friends and family.

LIGHT PREFERENCE: Give this plant bright light. If you have a place on your south or west windowsill, they will grow well. If placed in direct, unobstructed light, you may see it flower. If summered outside, they can sunburn, so acclimate them first, gradually moving them to high light.

WATERING: This juicy succulent does not need a lot of water, so keep the medium on the dry side. Make sure your aloe is in a fast-draining porous medium and never leave it standing in water.

FLOWER: With enough light, long stems and yellow tubular flowers will appear. It is unlikely that they will flower in your home.

SIZE: The leaves may reach up to 2 feet tall.

PROPAGATION: Aloes send out large numbers of "babies" or offsets at the base of the parent plant. They can be easily separated from the mother and potted up individually.

ALUMINUM PLANT

BOTANICAL NAME: *PILEA CADIERI*

The aluminum plant is named for its shiny, quilted leaves. The surface splotches are a shiny silver and look like aluminum. The colorful leaves of the pileas add a welcome respite to an all-green grouping of plants. If your plant gets leggy, as they often do, take cuttings and start new plants.

LIGHT PREFERENCE: Keep it in bright light, such as in an east or west window. It does not like full sun.

SIZE: It usually reaches 12 to 15 inches.

WATERING: Keep it evenly moist, never standing in water, and plant in a well-drained potting medium. Keep the humidity up by setting the plant on a pebble tray. With enough light, this plant will do well in a terrarium.

FLOWER: It does produce small clusters of white flowers held a couple of inches above the foliage. It may not bloom in your home environment, but is grown for its foliage anyway.

PROPAGATION: Pilea is easily propagated from tip cuttings rooted in moist potting medium.

ARROWHEAD VINE

BOTANICAL NAME: *SYNGONIUM PODOPHYLLUM*

When you purchase this plant, it may not be apparent that it is a vine. This characteristic may take a while to develop. Its most attractive factor is its arrowhead-shaped leaves that may range in color from silver to green to pink and any or all of those colors mixed together. It is an easy plant to grow.

LIGHT PREFERENCE: Place in a bright light and turn frequently as it tends to lean toward the light in a short span of time. The thin leaves will not appreciate an overly bright light, as they may sunburn.

WATERING: Keep the arrowhead evenly moist and place on a pebble tray for extra humidity. Allowing the plant to dry out or allowing the humidity to drop too low may cause the leaf edges and tips to brown.

FLOWER: They may develop a small white spadix or small spike of flowers surrounded by a white spathe or sheathing bract, but rarely in the home.

SIZE: Until it begins to vine, the plant is only 12 to 18 inches tall. Once it starts vining, it could reach up to 3 feet. They can be trained to grow up a mossy pole or trellis or can be trimmed to keep it smaller.

PROPAGATION: Take 6- to 8-inch tip cuttings and root in a moist potting medium. Because of their thin leaves and love of humidity, covering the cuttings while rooting may be helpful.

CULTIVARS:

• **'MOONSHINE'**—This variety is a light silver in color.

• **'WHITE BUTTERFLY'**—One of the most popular varieties available, with light green leaves edged in dark green.

• **'PINK SPLASH'**—A variety with pink markings scattered on medium green leaves.

• **'MINI PIXIE'**—A miniature white and green variety that may only grow to 3 inches, perfect for a terrarium or fairy garden.

• **'PINK FAIRY'**—A miniature variety that is pink in color and stays approximately 3 inches tall.

BABY RUBBER PLANT

BOTANICAL NAME: *PEPEROMIA OBTUSIFOLIA*

The name leads one to believe we are talking about a rubber plant (or ficus), but the two aren't related. This member of the Piperaceae family is a true succulent plant and can take some neglect, unlike its other family members. It has small, rounded, rubbery leaves, and it also has a variegated version that is attractive.

LIGHT PREFERENCE: They prefer medium to bright light, which is especially important if the plant is variegated.

WATERING: Use a fast-draining potting medium for this succulent plant. Water thoroughly, then water again when it is quite dry.

FLOWER: The flowers are on a long, skinny 2- to 3-inch-long spike resembling a rat tail. They are natural to the plant but hardly "attractive."

SIZE: It is rarely taller than 12 inches.

PROPAGATION: Propagate by taking stem cuttings, or it can be propagated from a single leaf, like the African violet.

CULTIVAR:

• **RAINBOW PEPEROMIA (*PEPEROMIA CLUSIIFOLIA*)**—This peperomia resembles the baby rubber plant and is in the same family. This one has more pointed leaves and red color in the leaves. The care is essentially the same.

BIRD'S NEST SNAKE PLANT

BOTANICAL NAME: *SANSEVIERIA TRIFASCIATA* 'Hahnii'

The snake plant, or mother-in-law's tongue, is easily identified by its tall, spiky leaves. Yet there is another type of snake plant that forms short rosettes of leaves resembling the round shape of bird's nests, thus the common name. They come in a range of colors from dark green to bright yellow, some with stripes and patches of variegation. These small plants are perfect for low-light and medium-light situations. The more variegation that is present on the leaves, the more light it will need to keep the colors vibrant.

LIGHT PREFERENCE: Snake plants are known for their tolerance of low light, especially the dark green varieties. If given a medium to bright light, they will do better.

WATERING: Keep this plant on the dry side, especially if it is placed in a low-light situation. If kept too wet, the plant will collapse due to rot. Do not leave water standing in the middle of the rosette for the same reason. If kept in medium to bright light, water when the planting medium is almost completely dry.

FLOWER: Older plants in enough light will send out a spray of white flowers, but that doesn't always happen in the conditions of a home setting.

SIZE: The bird's nest types can range from 4 inches to more than a foot high. They will expand and spread out with the growth of the offsets from the base of the parent plant.

PROPAGATION: The easiest way to propagate this plant is to separate the offsets and plant them in their own container. A single leaf can also be cut into pieces, allowed to callus over and be planted in a moist media. Make sure the leaf is placed so that the original bottom of the leaf is in the media or it will not grow.

CULTIVARS:

- **'GOLDEN HAHNII'**—A golden variety with stripes of lighter yellow and green. This plant will not exceed 5 inches in height, but after a few years will send out offsets and may reach 8 to 10 inches around and more if not separated.

- **'BLACK STAR'**—The leaves are a dark green edged with yellow.

- **'JADE'**—A pure dark green variety.

- **'STARLITE'**—A gray leaf edged with yellow.

BISHOP'S CAP CACTUS OR STAR PLANT

BOTANICAL NAME: *ASTROPHYTUM ORNATUM*

From above, this cactus has a star shape that appears to spiral a bit. It's easy to grow, and the white felt scales on the body of the cactus give the plant a unique look. It is globe-shaped as a young plant, but elongates with age. Make sure it is growing in a fast-draining medium to avoid rot.

LIGHT PREFERENCE: Give it a bright light such as a south-facing windowsill. If the light level is too low, the cactus will elongate excessively.

WATERING: Do not overwater this plant or allow it to sit in water. Too much water, or watering while the plant is sitting in a colder area, such as a windowsill, will cause the cactus to rot.

FLOWER: A pale yellow flower appears at the tip of this cactus, but may not do so in the home environment.

SIZE: With age, it can become as tall as 30 inches or more, but most likely will not reach that size in the house.

PROPAGATION: Propagate by sowing seed (if not from the flowers of another plant, then purchased from a reputable seed supplier).

BUNNY'S EARS, POLKA DOT CACTUS

BOTANICAL NAME: *OPUNTIA MICRODASYS*

This cute cactus may seem cuddly, as its names imply, but do not touch it without gloves. The spikes are really glochids that are very small barbed prickles. They attach to the skin and are quite painful; you may need tweezers to remove them. Many people use tape to pull them off or spread glue on the area, let it dry, and pull it off to remove the painful spikes. So why grow this plant? It is an endearing cactus, and the small tufts of glochids give it a polka-dot effect.

LIGHT PREFERENCE: Give this cactus as much light as you can, as it needs bright light to bloom.

WATERING: Plant this cactus in a well-drained soil. Water thoroughly and then allow the medium to dry down quite a bit before watering again. Do not allow the plant to stand in water. Keep it drier in the winter when the light levels are low.

FLOWER: The flowers are a creamy yellow and are borne on the tips of the "bunny ears."

SIZE: They are usually under 18 inches tall.

PROPAGATION: Carefully remove a pad of the plant, allow it to dry and callus over, and then plant in a well-drained medium.

CAST IRON PLANT

BOTANICAL NAME: *ASPIDISTRA ELATIOR*

This plant has been grown in dim parlors since the Victorian times, and as it tolerates low light and adverse conditions, it is known as the cast iron plant.

LIGHT PREFERENCE: It can tolerate low light but would do well in medium light. The newer variegated cultivars would need medium light to keep their variegation.

WATERING: It is also known for its tolerance to drying out, but would prefer to be evenly moist. The less light it has, the less water it will need.

FLOWER: The flowers are borne at the base of the leaves on the soil, but they are not often seen in the home setting.

SIZE: The long, strappy leaves can be up to 2½ feet long.

PROPAGATION: Separate sections of the plant and pot them up individually.

CULTIVARS:

- **'MILKY WAY'**—A speckled variety

- **'VARIEGATA'** —A white-striped variety

- **'SNOW CAP'** —This variety has white tips on the leaves.

CHINESE EVERGREEN

BOTANICAL NAME: *AGLAONEMA*

This group of plants is being hybridized at a rapid rate. They used to only be available in shades of green but now boast pinks, reds, and peach colors. An extremely easy plant to grow and now it is so much more beautiful.

LIGHT PREFERENCE: The older hybrids, mostly green, can take low light and grow quite well. The newer colorful hybrids need medium light and do well in an east or west window. If placed in low light, they will lose their bright coloration.

WATERING: Let the soil dry down 1 to 2 inches before watering. They would also prefer higher humidity, so place them on pebble trays.

FLOWER: *AGLAONEMA* with good light will flower, but as they are grown for their beautiful foliage, it benefits the plant to cut the flowers off. The flowering spadix is surrounded by a white spathe.

SIZE: The size ranges from 12 inches to approximately 3 feet.

PROPAGATION: *AGLAONEMA* can be propagated by stem cuttings or division.

CULTIVARS: These are just a few of the many cultivars now available. The newer ones have beautiful colors and markings.

- **'ANYANMANEE'** —Usually sold as Red Aglaonema in the stores, this cultivar has variegated dark pink leaves and grows 12 to 15 inches tall.

- **'CRETA'**—This cultivar has green leaves with red markings and grows 12 inches tall.

- **'EMERALD BEAUTY'**—This is one of the older varieties that can take low-light conditions. It has dark green leaves with light green mottled stripes and grows up to 24 inches tall.

- **'SILVER QUEEN'**—Also an older variety with opposite coloring of 'Emerald Beauty', this has light green leaves with dark green mottled stripes. It also can take lower light conditions and will grow up to 18 inches tall.

- **'PINK DALMATIAN'**—This is a beautiful cultivar with pink splashes on dark green shiny leaves. It grows 12 to 18 inches tall.

- **'WHITE LANCE'**—The leaves of this unusual cultivar are only 1 inch wide and have a light gray color. It grows 18 inches tall.

- **'SPARKLING SARAH'**—This cultivar, which grows 12 to 15 inches tall, sports a pink midrib with pink veins on a bright green leaf.

COPPER SPOONS

BOTANICAL NAME: *KALANCHOE ORGYALIS*

The leaves of this unique plant are covered with a brown-colored fuzz that feels like velvet. As it ages, the color fades to a silver color. It is definitely a conversation piece if grown in a bright window, which gives it the best color. This is a great plant for kids, as they love to pet the soft leaves.

LIGHT PREFERENCE: Grow this colorful succulent in a south or west window for the best color and more compact growth. If grown in light that is too low, the plant will stretch and reach for the light.

WATERING: Grow in a fast-draining medium as this succulent plant does not want to be waterlogged. After watering, let it almost completely dry out before watering again.

FLOWER: If given enough light, it may produce small, bright yellow flowers at the tip of the plant.

SIZE: It can grow up to 4 feet tall, but in the home may stay quite a bit smaller.

PROPAGATION: Take tip cuttings but allow them to callus over before planting in a moist, fast-draining potting medium.

CROWN OF THORNS

BOTANICAL NAME: *EUPHORBIA MILII*

Though this plant has many spines, it is not a cactus; it's a succulent member of the spurge family. The spines may be hard to see as they are hidden by many oblong leaves. The common name comes from the fanciful idea that the crown of thorns Jesus wore may have been made out of these plants.

The crown of thorns has come a long way in the last few years with many new hybrids. There are Thai hybrids that have bracts (modified leaves) and flowers that resemble hydrangea heads and are quite large. The colors of the bracts, formerly only red, now come in myriad colors including pink, green, bicolor, splotched, and more. These cousins of poinsettias also have tiny flowers surrounded by colorful bracts that are much larger than the actual flowers. Take care when handling this plant, not only because of the many spines, but because the plant has a white sap that can be irritating. Do not get it in your mouth or eyes.

LIGHT PREFERENCE: Give these plants as much light as you can. A south or west window would be best.

WATERING: Do not let these succulents completely dry out. If allowed to dry out, the leaves will yellow and fall off. If that happens, as soon as water is applied, they should regrow leaves. Grow in a fast-draining potting medium.

FLOWER: As previously mentioned, the true flowers are very small, but surrounded by colorful bracts ranging from yellow to pink, red, and more. Depending on the light, moisture, and warmth, these plants may bloom on and off all year.

SIZE: There are miniature plants that may only reach a few inches to plants that may reach over 3 feet in the home setting.

PROPAGATION: Tip cuttings can be taken and placed in a moist potting medium.

CULTIVARS:

- **'NORTHERN LIGHTS'**—The variegated leaves of this cultivar make it a stand out. It still has the red bracts surrounding the flowers.

- **'PINK CADILLAC'**—The bright pink bracts surrounding the flowers stand out against the large, oblong, bright green leaves.

- **'LEMON DROP'**—A miniature plant with small yellow bracts perfect for small dish gardens.

- **'SPLENDENS'**—A miniature plant with small red bracts. Perfect for a fairy garden.

DRACAENA

BOTANICAL NAME: *DRACAENA DEREMENSIS*

Dracaenas are some of the most popular and easiest houseplants to grow. They thrive in a medium to bright light but do quite well in low-light conditions. The hybrid 'Janet Craig' is most often used as a low-light plant in commercial settings, but is a nice houseplant for a low-light home setting as well. The fountain-like look of the dark green leaves makes a nice statement in a low-light corner or it can cover a bare spot that needs some life. The variegated varieties would need a much brighter place to keep their color. The leaves get dusty quickly, so either give the plant a shower when necessary or wipe down the leaves often.

LIGHT PREFERENCE: As previously discussed, these plants are quite tolerant of low-light levels, but would prefer a medium light to really thrive.

WATERING: The dracaenas as a group do not like to be overly wet, but evenly moist. They are sensitive to fluoride in tap water, so if your metropolitan water has this chemical added, using rainwater or bottled water will prevent the plant tips from browning.

FLOWER: A stem of white flowers can sprout from among the leaves, but most often will not be seen in the home setting.

SIZE: These plants can reach large proportions, but most likely won't grow to more than 10 feet in your home and that after many years. To keep it smaller, you can cut the tops off, rooting them in the same pot or starting them in another container.

PROPAGATION: Propagate by taking cuttings and rooting them in moist potting medium. This is the easiest method, but air layering (see page 34) could be used as well.

CULTIVARS:

- **'JANET CRAIG COMPACTA'**—This small version of Janet Craig has leaves usually not more than 5 to 6 inches long, and the growth is very compact with the individual stems of leaves only reaching 10 inches across. This plant is quite slow growing.

- **'DORADO'**—A dark green cultivar with dark green leaves and thin chartreuse edges.

- **'LEMON LIME'** (above)—Green leaves with yellow edges and a white strip down the middle. Beautiful variegated form.

- **'LEMON SURPRISE'**—With similar variegation to 'Lemon Lime' except with a slight twist in the leaves for added interest.

- **'LIMELIGHT'**—A completely bright chartreuse color that adds a bright accent to any area.

- **'RIKKI'**—These thinner than most, dark green leaves have a light green stripe down the middle.

- **'WARNECKII'**—This older variety sports green leaves with stripes of darker green and white.

DRAGON TREE

BOTANICAL NAME: *DRACAENA MARGINATA*

These strappy-leaved houseplants are very popular with humans and, unfortunately, kitties enjoy nibbling on them as well; the leaves must remind them of large grass blades. The plants can become very picturesque with age as their trunks can become twisted and contorted. The stems, though uniquely shaped, will have tufts of foliage at the ends only. If they become too large for the house, they can be trimmed back and the cut ends rooted. It will take years for a small plant to become overly large.

LIGHT PREFERENCE: Though these plants can tolerate low-light levels, they would prefer a medium to bright light. If the plant is variegated, which they quite often are, they will need a more intense light to keep the color.

WATERING: Keep the medium evenly moist during the growing season, but drier during the darker, cooler winter months. If this plant is overwatered, the canes will rot.

FLOWER: It does produce fragrant white flowers, but likely not in the home setting.

SIZE: When mature, they may reach upward of 10 feet.

PROPAGATION: The stem tips can be clipped off and placed in a moist potting media to root. The stem that has had the top cut off will sprout new growth with time. This works well when the plant has become too tall. The top can be cut back drastically and the resprouting cane will start out shorter. Air layering would work as well, but would be a much slower process. Stem cuttings (without foliage) can also be taken and planted; make sure the bottom end of the cane is in the potting media.

CULTIVARS:

- **'COLORAMA'**—This newer cultivar appears to be a purely bright pink plant when in reality it is variegated with white and green. The color is stunning and will need a very bright light to keep the striking color bright.

- **'TRICOLOR'**—This older but still beautiful cultivar has three colors in its leaves including green, white, and dark pink/red.

DUMB CANE

BOTANICAL NAME: *DIEFFENBACHIA SEGUINE*

The main feature of this plant is the attractive foliage. The common name comes from the fact that the plant sap contains calcium oxalate crystals that can burn the mouth and throat and may cause a temporary paralysis of the vocal chords. Keep this plant away from children and pets. The large leaves boast splotches and patches of darker green or white, making it a beautiful foliage plant.

LIGHT PREFERENCE: Place in a medium to bright light such as in an east or west window.

WATERING: Keep this plant evenly moist and raise the humidity by placing the container on a pebble tray.

FLOWER: White flowers followed by red berries will most likely not appear on plants in a home setting.

SIZE: There are many cultivars ranging from under 1 foot tall to 4 to 5 feet tall.

PROPAGATION: Cut the top few inches off a stem and root in a moist medium. The stems or canes can be cut into pieces, each with a node, and laid horizontally on a moist medium to root.

CULTIVARS: There are too many to list, but here are a few striking varieties to look for:

- **'CAMILLE'**—A bright chartreuse leaf with dark green edges.

- **'CAMOUFLAGE'**—A bright chartreuse leaf with splotches of dark green scattered over the leaf.

- **'STERLING'**—A medium-sized plant with a dark green leaf that has a chartreuse green midrib and veins running through it.

- **'TROPIC SNOW'** —This large variety can grow to 5 feet or more in height and has a bright green leaf with a yellow middle feathering into the green edges.

- **'TROPIC HONEY'**—This large variety has all yellow leaves with a thick, dark green edge.

DWARF ALOES

BOTANICAL NAME: *ALOE* sp.

These small cultivars are newer and have taken the succulent world by storm. They are small, colorful, and not too spiky. They stay under 5 inches and form many offsets, making them easy to propagate and share. They are often sold in the spring at garden centers for combination dish gardens, but make good houseplants with enough light. A few cultivars are mentioned below, but there are numerous others.

LIGHT PREFERENCE: Give these plants as much light as you can to keep them compact and colorful. If they have lots of light, they will produce more offsets.

WATERING: Water thoroughly and then allow the potting medium to dry out a bit so as not to rot them. If they become too dry, the plant edges will curl.

FLOWER: These plants will have colorful flowers, usually in the orange range, but most likely will not bloom in the house.

SIZE: Small rosettes usually a few inches tall and wide.

PROPAGATION: Separate the offsets from the parent and pot up individually.

CULTIVARS:

- **'BLIZZARD'**—A version that has so many white tubercles on the green leaves, they are almost all white.

- **'DORAN BLACK'**—A dark chocolate-colored leaf covered with white spots.

- **'PINK BLUSH'**—Green leaves covered with oblong tubercles with pink edges.

DYCKIA BROMELIAD

As spiny as the edges of the leaves of dyckia are, one could mistake it as being related to the cactus family. In reality, it is a bromeliad, related to the air plants or tillandsias, and the fruit-bearing pineapple plant. They aren't epiphytes as the tillandsias are, though, but terrestrial like the pineapple plant, growing primarily on the ground. When handling these plants, wear gloves, as the spines can be painful. They are an unusual plant with many colorful varieties.

LIGHT PREFERENCE: Dyckias would prefer full sun, so a south window is best in the home setting.

WATERING: Dyckias need to be in a well-drained potting medium. Do not overwater; be especially careful of this in the lower light times of the year.

FLOWER: They produce orange or yellow flowers, pollinated by hummingbirds in their native habitat. Flowers will most likely not appear in the home setting unless the light is exceptionally high.

SIZE: They range in size from 6 inches to 3 feet across and range from a few inches to foot or more tall.

PROPAGATION: These plants multiply by offsets at the base of the parent plant. When they are a good size, they can be separated and potted up individually. This process will require gloves to protect hands from the spines on the leaves.

CULTIVARS:

- **'BRITTLE STAR'**—This very attractive plant is grayish white with a burgundy midrib.

- **'CHERRY COLA'**—This newer hybrid has shiny dark red leaves.

- **'NAKED LADY'**—The name is as it implies. The green leaves have no spines at all.

FAIRY WASHBOARD

BOTANICAL NAME: *HAWORTHIA LIMIFOLIA*

Haworthias are the perfect succulents for our homes as they need less light than most succulents, which need full sun. The flower grows in a small rosette, and each leaf has ridges protruding from the surface, giving it its common name. This small succulent rarely reaches more than 4 inches across, making it ideal for an indoor fairy garden, especially given its name.

LIGHT PREFERENCE: Place this succulent in a medium to bright light. Do not give it the full sun other succulents prefer, as it will turn to burgundy and may sunburn.

WATERING: These succulents need the potting medium to become almost completely dry before watering again, especially if they are growing in a lower light level.

FLOWER: The flower stalk will appear from the center of the rosette and may extend over 2 feet long with small, white, trumpet-shaped flowers.

SIZE: The small rosette of leaves will be approximately 2 inches tall and not more than 4 inches wide.

PROPAGATION: Remove offsets from the base of the plant and pot up individually.

CULTIVARS: A variegated form of this plant is worth the search, as it is beautiful, but it is not easy to find and may be costly.

- *HAWORTHIA LIMIFOLIA* var. *stricta*—The ridges on this variety are white.

FIRE FLASH SPIDER PLANT

BOTANICAL NAME: *CHLOROPHYTUM AMANIENSE* 'Fire Flash'

This colorful relative of the much-loved spider or airplane plant in no way resembles its cousin. Vibrant orange petioles hold up dark green leaves, providing a beautiful contrast. It sends up white flower spikes covered with flowers that resemble those of the spider plant.

LIGHT PREFERENCE: To keep its bright orange color, it needs a medium-light situation as in an east window. In general, this is a houseplant that will thrive on less light rather than more, a trait it shares with the peace lily (or spathiphyllum). Too much light will cause the foliage to look bleached and pale.

WATERING: Keep the 'Fire Flash' evenly moist. It would prefer water without fluoride as fluoride will burn the tips of the plants.

FLOWER: The white flowers appear on a short stalk that arises from the middle of the plant. If left on the plant, it will produce seedpods; when they open and fall into the container, they will sprout new babies.

PROPAGATION: Collect the seeds after blooming and sow in a moist medium, or wait for the seeds to sprout in the container and pot up the babies individually.

FLAME VIOLET

BOTANICAL NAME: *EPISCIA* sp.

The flame violet is so called for its bright red flowers and the fact that it is related to the African violet. They are both in the Gesneriad family. It is primarily grown for its colorful, vibrant foliage. These plants love warmth and humidity, making them perfect for terrarium culture. They grow an abundance of stolons or runners (like a strawberry plant), so they are well suited to a hanging basket and, in fact, that is how they are usually offered for sale.

LIGHT PREFERENCE: It prefers a bright but indirect light. An east window is perfect, but it can also be grown under electric lights.

WATERING: Keep the episcia evenly moist and raise the humidity around the plant by placing the container on a pebble tray.

FLOWER: The tubular flowers may be white, yellow, lavender, pink, or red, depending on the variety.

SIZE: Whereas the plant is only a few inches tall, if left to spread, it can grow to 18 inches wide or more.

PROPAGATION: New episcia can be grown from the small plantlets at the end of the runners.

GASTERALOE 'LITTLE WARTY'

Gasteraloes are a cross between the genera gasteria and aloe. They form a rosette of stiff succulent leaves. The stripes of green and white and the warty texture make for an interesting succulent. Its ease of care and medium-light requirements add to the popularity of this plant.

LIGHT PREFERENCE: A bright to medium light such as an east or west window is best.

WATERING: Plant this succulent in a fast-draining potting medium. It needs water when the medium is almost completely dry.

FLOWER: The flowers have the color of gasteria flowers, usually orange with green, but have the shape of the aloe flower, which is tubular. The little stomach shape apparent in the gasteria genus is not present on the gasteraloe.

SIZE: The plant will spread sideways as it multiplies by offsets. It will only reach 4 to 5 inches in height.

PROPAGATION: Separate the offsets from the parent plant and pot them up individually.

GASTERIA BICOLOR VAR. *LILIPUTANA*

GOLDEN BARREL CACTUS

This tiny gasteria rarely gets taller than an inch or two, and it may never need a container larger than 3 to 4 inches around. It's a small succulent that can reside on a windowsill, but only needs medium light. It is perfect for an indoor fairy garden.

LIGHT PREFERENCE: The gasterias as a group really only need a medium light compared to most full sun succulents. If it is a variegated plant, it will need a little more light to keep its variegation.

WATERING: As these are succulents, they need to be planted in a fast-draining potting medium and watered only when the medium is almost completely dry.

SIZE: This tiny variety is only an inch or two tall and can become 2 to 3 inches across as it produces many offsets.

PROPAGATION: Separate the offsets from the parent plant and pot them up individually.

BOTANICAL NAME: *ECHINOCACTUS GRUSONII*

These iconic cacti are most often seen in conservatories and are endangered in their native Mexico. There, they are said to naturally slant slightly to the south, like living compasses. The golden spines and globe shape of these plants make for a striking specimen and one well suited for full sun areas. The spikes are plentiful and so they must be handled with extreme care when moving or repotting. As the plant ages, it will become more oblong than round.

LIGHT PREFERENCE: In your home, give the barrel cactus as much light as possible. Close to an unobstructed south window would be best.

WATERING: In the house, don't let the medium completely dry out, especially in the summer when it is actively growing. In the winter, the water should be applied sparingly, if at all. If it is in a cool room, do not water as it may rot the plant.

FLOWER: This plant produces yellow flowers, but most likely it will not bloom in the home environment.

SIZE: The barrel cactus may reach 1 to 3 feet tall in the house.

PROPAGATION: These can be propagated from seeds.

GOLDFISH PLANT

BOTANICAL NAME: *NEMATANTHUS GREGARIUS*

The flowers of this vining plant resemble small orange fish. It is a cousin of African violets but tends to epiphytic in its natural habitat; it is most often sold in hanging baskets.

LIGHT PREFERENCE: To expect the cute, goldfish-like flowers to appear, a medium to bright light is needed. An east or west window is sufficient, or grow them under electric lights to ensure blooms.

WATERING: Keep this plant evenly moist, especially while blooming, to keep the flowers looking their best.

FLOWER: With the correct light, these plants could have flowers year-round.

SIZE: The goldfish plant is often offered as a hanging basket and is only a few inches high, but the stems may hang 12 to 15 inches down from the edge of the basket.

PROPAGATION: Take tip cuttings a few inches long and insert them into a moist potting medium.

CULTIVARS:

• **'BLACK GOLD'**—A cultivar with dark green, almost-burgundy foliage that makes the golden flowers more obvious.

• **'TROPICANA'**—The flowers of this cultivar have burgundy lines running through the orange flowers.

• **'VARIEGATA'**—The leaves are green and cream.

GRAPE IVY

BOTANICAL NAME: *CISSUS RHOMBIFOLIA* 'Ellen Danica'

A vining plant, grape ivy is a perfect plant for a trellis or hanging basket. It has dark green leaves that are separated into leaflets, which resemble small oak leaves rather than grape leaves. It's a robust plant that can cover a problem spot or a dark corner quickly.

LIGHT PREFERENCE: This is a versatile vine that can tolerate a low-light north window but would prefer a medium light in an east or west window.

WATERING: Plant in a peat-based but well-drained medium, and keep the plant evenly moist. Do not allow it to stand in water, but if it dries out, it will drop leaves.

SIZE: This vine can reach lengths of 10 to 12 feet. Trim to keep it a more manageable size if needed.

PROPAGATION: Take tip cuttings and root in a moist potting medium.

HEARTLEAF PHILODENDRON

BOTANICAL NAME: *PHILODENDRON HEDERACEUM*

The heartleaf philodendron is undeniably the most loved houseplant of all time. The heart-shaped leaves and ease of care account for its popularity. Many a window has been framed by this endearing vine. The newer cultivars have kept its popularity high.

LIGHT PREFERENCE: This philodendron can survive in low light but will thrive in medium light, such as an east or west window.

WATERING: This is a forgiving plant if it dries out, but it would prefer to be kept evenly moist. It does not want to be wet, though.

FLOWER: It is grown for its foliage.

SIZE: This trailing plant can get quite long, but it can be kept bushy by trimming some of the stems back to the soil line. New shoots will emerge.

PROPAGATION: Take stem tip cuttings and pot in a moist potting medium.

CULTIVARS:

- **'LEMON LIME'**—Bright green leaves.

- **'BRASIL'**—Dark green leaves with bright green stripes.

- *PHILODENDRON BRANDTIANUM*—Gray leaves with dark green veins.

HENS AND CHICKS

BOTANICAL NAME: *ECHEVERIA* sp.

Echeverias are tropical hens and chicks and are quite often mistaken for sempervivums, their hardy northern look-alikes. Echeverias, on the other hand, would like to be kept warm and given plenty of light. If exposed to freezing temperatures, they may die. These succulents come in many different forms and colors. If you have a high-light window, these would be perfect.

LIGHT PREFERENCE: Choose the brightest spot in the house, such as a south-facing windowsill. If in too low a light, these succulents will stretch for the light. They may still stretch even in an unobstructed south window, so in winter will benefit from being grown under electric lights.

WATERING: These succulents need a fast-draining potting medium. Water thoroughly and then let the medium almost dry out before watering again. In the winter, wait longer to water than you did in the growing season.

FLOWER: The flowers of echeverias are usually orange or yellow and are held on arching stems about 1 foot above the foliage.

SIZE: There are small varieties that are inches across to large varieties that can be 2 feet across.

PROPAGATION: Echeverias make offsets which can be separated and potted up individually. Echeverias can also be propagated by individual leaves. Pull a leaf off, let the end callus over, and then lay on top of a moist medium. Small plantlets will form at the end of the leaf. The whole plant can be cut off its stem and laid on to of a container of potting medium, and it will form roots. The naked stem that the head was cut off of may sprout new plantlets that can also be removed and potted.

CULTIVARS: There are so many cultivars to choose from. Here are just a few:

- **'BLACK PRINCE'**—This is a cultivar with dark burgundy leaves.

- **'PERLE VON NURNBERG'**—A purplish-gray sheen is the main feature of this cultivar.

- **'TOPSY TURVY'**—The gray color of this popular cultivar isn't too memorable, but the shape of the leaves is. They turn up at the ends and come to a point.

- ***ECHEVERIA SHAVIANA* 'ROSEA'**—This cultivar has ruffled edges on a blue-colored plant with purple shading. A showstopper!

JEWEL ORCHID

BOTANICAL NAME: *LUDISIA DISCOLOR*

This terrestrial orchid is grown for its beautiful foliage more than for its spikes of white flowers. The burgundy foliage has iridescent peach stripes. This is an extremely easy orchid to grow in potting medium and achieve bloom in a medium-light window. These plants can become leggy as they get older. Take tip cuttings and after rooting them, plant them back in the pot to help the plant stay fuller and more attractive.

LIGHT PREFERENCE: These orchids are found in shady places in their native habitat, so they are perfect for our homes. They do need a bright light to bloom, though, so give them a medium light, such as an east window. Turn your plant regularly to promote flowering on the entire plant.

WATERING: Keep the medium evenly moist and plant in a heavy, peat-based potting medium.

FLOWER: The small flowers are white and appear on flower stems that rise above the foliage approximately 12 inches.

SIZE: The foliage is only a few inches high but the stems do extend over the edge of the pot and hang down approximately 8 to 10 inches. These plants would make an excellent hanging basket.

PROPAGATION: Tip cuttings are easily rooted in moist potting medium. The plant could also be cut apart and pieces potted up individually.

LIFESAVER PLANT

BOTANICAL NAME: *HUERNIA ZEBRINA*

A unique flower gives rise to the name lifesaver plant. The center of the flower does look like a shiny, burgundy inner tube or lifesaver. It's a succulent, easy to grow and bloom in a bright light.

LIGHT PREFERENCE: A south or west window will provide enough light to get this show-stopping plant to bloom.

WATERING: Keep this succulent on the dry side but do not let it dry out completely, especially when in flower.

FLOWER: The unassuming plant doesn't wow, but the unique flower will. It's shaped like a burgundy, rubber lifesaver with burgundy-speckled, cream-colored triangular petals surrounding it. The flower is approximately 1 inch across.

SIZE: This small, 3- to 4-inch succulent can spread out as wide as the container it is growing in. A short wide container, such as a bulb pan, with drainage would be perfect.

PROPAGATION: Stem cuttings will root in a moist potting medium after the cuttings are allowed to callus over.

LIPSTICK PLANT

BOTANICAL NAME: *AESCHYNANTHUS RADICANS*

The lipstick plant is so named for the beautiful, bright reddish-orange flowers that appear as if they are rising out of a tube of lipstick. Usually sold as hanging baskets, these plants are cousins of African violets in the Gesneriad family and like similar growing conditions. Hang them in an east or west window and be sure to turn them often to ensure blooms on all sides of the plant.

LIGHT PREFERENCE: Grow in an east or west window or under electric lights for the most blooms. Turn the plant often if growing in a window to ensure equal blooms on all sides.

WATERING: Keep the plant evenly moist. These plants are quite often grown in a mix with a large amount of peat, so if the plant is allowed to dry out, it is hard to re-wet the medium. To prevent rot, do not let the plant stand in water.

FLOWER: The red flowers emerge from calyxes (sepals of a flower) giving the appearance of a lipstick emerging from its container.

SIZE: This vine is 12 to 24 inches long.

PROPAGATION: Take tip cuttings and pot in a moist potting medium.

CULTIVARS:

• **'TANGERINE'**—Dark green foliage with yellow flowers.

• **'VARIEGATA'**—White variegation in the leaves with red-orange flowers.

• **'RASTA'**—The curled foliage gives this cultivar its interest.

LUCKY BAMBOO

BOTANICAL NAME: *DRACAENA SANDERIANA*

Lucky bamboo, which is not a bamboo at all, has been popular since it first came to the market in the late 1990s. It is said to bring luck and is used extensively in feng shui. If the stem curls, it has been trained that way by using phototropism to make the plant grow and turn toward light. This is an easy plant to grow in water only, which is how it often offered for sale.

LIGHT PREFERENCE: Place this plant in bright light. Full sun would be too much for it, so place it in an east window or back a few feet from a south or west window.

WATERING: This plant is most often grown exclusively in water, but it can be grown in a potting medium as well. Dracaenas do not like the chemicals in tap water, so use rain water or distilled water if possible. Change the water at least one to two times per month, and keep the water at the same level all the time. If grown in soil, keep it evenly moist.

FLOWER: It's not likely to flower in the home.

SIZE: These canes can be only an inch tall to many feet tall. They can be kept trimmed.

PROPAGATION: Cuttings can be taken and rooted in moist potting medium or placed in water to grow roots. If you cut the top of the cane off, new sprouts will emerge lower on the cane. The cane piece that has been cut off, if it still has green leaves attached, can be placed in water to grow new roots.

MADAGASCAR PALM

BOTANICAL NAME: *PACHYPODIUM LAMEREI*

The Madagascar palm is not a palm at all but is a succulent with spines. The leaves mostly grow on the top of the stem, giving it a palm-like look. The stem has a silver color, further adding to its beauty.

LIGHT PREFERENCE: Give this plant as much light as possible. It will stretch if not given enough light.

WATERING: Plant in a fast-draining potting medium and after watering thoroughly, let the medium dry down quite a bit before watering again. Overwatering or allowing the plant to stand in water will rot it.

FLOWER: It does produce white flowers at the top of the plant, but most likely will not flower in the home setting.

SIZE: It could reach 18 to 20 feet in its natural habitat, but usually only reaches less than 6 feet in the home.

PROPAGATION: Take a cutting and allow it to callus over before planting in a moist potting medium.

MINI MONSTERA VINE

BOTANICAL NAME: *RHAPHIDOPHORA TETRASPERMA*

This vining plant resembles (and is related to) the Swiss cheese plant **MONSTERA DELICIOSA**, but the leaves will only ever achieve a size of 6 inches. It's easy to grow and can tolerate low light.

LIGHT PREFERENCE: It would like a medium light, but can tolerate low light. A north, east, or west window would work well. No direct sun is needed, as too much light can cause the leaves to bleach.

WATERING: Keep the potting medium evenly moist. If the plant is in low light, it will need less water.

FLOWER: It most likely will not flower in the home.

SIZE: This vine can grow 6 to 10 feet in length.

PROPAGATION: Stem cuttings can be rooted in a moist potting medium.

MINI UMBRELLA TREE

BOTANICAL NAME: *SCHEFFLERA ARBORICOLA*

This plant is the mini version of the umbrella tree, **SCHEFFLERA ACTINOPHYLLA**. Seven to nine leaflets arranged in a whorl on short stems cover this small shrub-like plant. The leaves are bright green, and most often the variegated versions are the ones offered for sale.

LIGHT PREFERENCE: Give it a medium to bright light. The variegated versions need more light than the all-green ones.

WATERING: Water thoroughly and then allow the medium to dry down a bit before watering again. It is easy to rot this plant, so keeping it on the drier side is better than keeping it wet. Keep it drier in the winter when the light levels are lower.

FLOWER: It does have tiny red flowers but most likely will not have them in the house.

SIZE: In its native habitat, this plant can be 10 to 25 feet tall, but in the home it may be 3 to 6 feet tall.

PROPAGATION: Take tip cuttings and root in moist potting medium.

CULTIVARS:

• **'DAZZLE'**—This variety is variegated with white.

• **'GOLD CAPELLA'**—This variety is variegated with yellow.

MISTLETOE CACTUS

BOTANICAL NAME: *RHIPSALIS*

Called the mistletoe cactus for its appearance and its habit of hanging out in trees, this plant grows as an epiphyte. It is a cactus, but a tropical rainforest one, not the typical desert variety. You won't notice any spines, but a few do have bristles. The small cream to white flowers turn into white berries, furthering the mistletoe resemblance. They have a tendency to have a weeping form and so are most often sold in hanging baskets.

LIGHT PREFERENCE: This is a plant that can take less light then most cacti. A bright light and high humidity, which mimics their natural habitat, is best. Hang in a south or west window for the best results.

WATERING: Water thoroughly and then allow the plant to dry a bit before watering again. Too much water will rot this plant, yet on the other hand, if under-watered, pieces of the plants will begin to fall off.

FLOWER: Small white, cream, or yellow flowers may appear on this plant if it is exposed to enough light.

SIZE: Whether in a regular pot or a hanging basket, the branches may cascade a foot or more over the sides of the container.

PROPAGATION: Cut off segments of the stems and allow the ends to callus over, then plant them in a moist potting medium.

MONEY TREE, GUIANA CHESTNUT

BOTANICAL NAME: *PACHIRA AQUATICA*

This popular plant has taken the last decade by storm. The feng shui movement brought pachira to the forefront as it is purported to bring good luck. The plant is usually sold with a braided trunk and the five to seven bright green leaflets that make up one leaf are unusual and beautiful. It is often sold as a bonsai as well. Its ease of care and low light tolerance also adds to the popularity. There is some confusion whether the plant most often sold is **PACHIRA AQUATIC** or **P. GLABRA**, but since the only way to tell the difference is by seeing the flower, we probably won't know because it is unlikely to flower in our homes.

LIGHT PREFERENCE: A medium to bright light is best, such as that offered by an east or west window.

WATERING: This plant grows in water in its native habitat, but as a houseplant, do not leave it standing in water. Keep the soil evenly moist.

FLOWER: Large, yellowish-white flowers have five recurving petals surrounding a shaving brush – like group of stamens with red tips. Each flower turns into a large woody pod, encasing a nut that is said to taste like a peanut. The flowers most likely will not appear in the home situation.

SIZE: In nature, this plant becomes a 50- to 60-foot tree, but can be kept to 6 to 8 feet in your home. Do not up-pot the tree when it gets to the size you would like to keep it. Instead, root prune it, trim the top, and return it to the same size container.

PROPAGATION: Take tip cuttings and root them in a moist potting medium.

MOTH ORCHID

BOTANICAL NAME: *PHALAENOPSIS*

Moth orchids were once attainable only to the wealthy. Tissue culture has made this gorgeous plant available to almost everyone. The cultivars and flower colors are endless and more are being hybridized every day. The only color they don't come in is blue. If you see the blue ones for sale they have been sprayed with vegetable dye and succeeding generations of flowers will be snow white. The flowers can last for months if the plant is cared for correctly, which means not allowing it to dry out or stand in water. The best part is how easy they are to bring into bloom again.

LIGHT PREFERENCE: Moth orchids need a medium to bright light to produce flowers. An east or west window is best.

FLOWER: The flowers have been named moth orchids in reference to their appearance, as they resemble moth wings. Once the flower stalk has appeared, the plant can be moved to any spot, because once the flowers are started, they don't need the same light to continue to bloom. The flowers can last for months as long as the plant isn't allowed to dry out or stand in water. When the flowers fade, the stem can be cut off at the base to allow the plant to put all its energy into growing and making a bigger and better display of flowers the next year. If you cut the stem above the second node (swollen area on the stem), it may send out another display of flowers.

WATERING: Take your plant to the sink, and remove it from the decorative pot or sleeve. Run water through the actual pot and then allow it to drain. Return to the decorative pot and to the spot it was growing. If water gets in the middle of the leaves, make sure to blot it out with a paper towel, as standing water may rot the plant.

SIZE: The plant itself is usually 6 to 8 inches tall and approximately 12 inches wide. The flower stems will rise above the plants 24 to 30 inches. There are also miniature moth orchids only a few inches high.

PROPAGATION: Occasionally, small plantlets called *keikis* appear on the flower stem at the nodes. Care for the plant as usual, allowing the small plantlets to grow larger. When they have roots a few inches long, cut from the parent and pot individually.

OLD MAN OF THE ANDES

BOTANICAL NAME: *OREOCEREUS CELSIANUS*

The white furry covering of this cactus gives it the common name along with the fact that it grows high in the Andes Mountains of South America. Its white covering is grown to protect it from sunburn. Do not let the cute woolly covering fool you, as it is very spiny underneath. If the "fur" becomes dusty or dirty, it can be washed, but would need to be a warm day and a place with good air circulation to completely dry it out.

LIGHT PREFERENCE: In the home, it would prefer bright light from a south or west windowsill.

WATERING: These plants need a fast-draining coarse mix to prevent root rot. Water very sparingly as these plants rot easily. They do not like high or low temperatures. The more sun they have, the denser the white hair becomes. Try not to water on an overcast day or a cold winter day.

FLOWER: It can produce tubular red flowers in the spring, but will likely not do that in our homes.

SIZE: These plants can reach heights of 10 feet in the mountains where they reside naturally. They grow slowly and may reach 1 to 2 feet or more in the house.

PROPAGATION: Sow seed to propagate.

OX-TONGUE

BOTANICAL NAME: *GASTERIA CARINATA* var. *VERRUCOSA*

Ox-tongue leaves are said by some to resemble a tongue. They do have a rounded tip and tubercles (small round protuberances) scattered over the leaves. They are easy to grow and make a great medium-light succulent houseplant. They can be placed in a lower light and still do well. The gasteria name comes from their flowers, which resemble the shape of a stomach. The plant will easily produce flowers on a west windowsill. This particular plant is a dark green with white tubercles all over the leaves.

LIGHT PREFERENCE: Gasterias can thrive on a west or east windowsill and, in fact, could be placed a few feet from a south window and do well.

WATERING: These fleshy succulents should be planted in a fast-draining medium and never be allowed to stand in water. Keep drier in the winter when the light levels are lower.

FLOWER: As mentioned before, the small flowers are shaped like a stomach. Most are orange with a green tip and hang from 2- to 3-foot-long stems.

SIZE: Gasterias can range from a little over 1 inch high to more than 2 feet tall.

PROPAGATION: They make quite a large number of offsets; these can be removed and potted up individually. They also can be started from seed. Single leaves can be removed, allowed to dry for a few weeks and planted in a moist potting mix. Or they can be laid horizontally on the medium, and they will grow babies and roots from the cut end in a few months.

PEACE LILY

BOTANICAL NAME: *SPATHIPHYLLUM*

Not a true lily, but related instead to the aglaonema, philodendron, and dieffenbachia, which are all aroids. These popular plants are easy to care for and forgiving of being allowed to wilt from under-watering. The white flowers appear with a medium light, which the plant prefers. The beautiful shiny dark green leaves make it more attractive.

LIGHT PREFERENCE: The peace lily can tolerate a medium to low light, but flowers may not appear in less than a medium light. An east or north window would work well, but the east window will produce flowers while the north may not. It will flower 5 to 6 feet away from a west window.

WATERING: This plant does not like to dry out, so keep it evenly moist. It will wilt from under-watering and come back quite well as soon as water is added to the medium. Some use the wilting as a visual indicator to water. Yet, if that happens often, leaves dying back from the tips will result. It is better to check it often and keep it moist.

FLOWER: While it would appear that the large, white, flag-like appendage is the flower of the peace lily, it is actually a spathe. The white upright cylinder that appears in the middle of the spathe is the spadix, and it is covered with tiny flowers. Pollen falls from them and can be seen on the leaves. Quite often in commercial settings, the spadix is removed to keep the leaves clean and pollen free. The flowers last for a long time, which is a nice bonus.

SIZE: Peace lilies have many cultivars ranging from 1 foot tall to over 4 feet tall.

PROPAGATION: The peace lily is a multiple crown plant. The easy way to propagate it is to just separate the crowns and plant them up individually.

CULTIVARS:

- **'DOMINO'**—A variegated form that has white markings on the puckered leaves.

PERUVIAN OLD LADY CACTUS

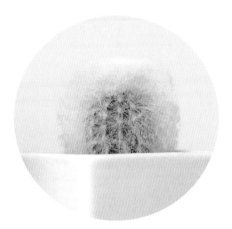

BOTANICAL NAME: *ESPOSTOA MELANOSTELE*

This mountain-dwelling cactus grows white "hair" to protect itself from the intense sun it encounters in its native habitat. To make sure there is plenty of the white hair on your specimen, place it in as much sun as possible. Don't let the furry look of this plant fool you. There are plenty of sharp spines under there. Overwatering this cactus is its biggest killer.

LIGHT PREFERENCE: A bright light is a must for this light-loving cactus. A south or west windowsill would be the best spot for it.

WATERING: This cactus needs a light hand with the watering can. This is especially important in the winter when light levels are low and it is cold on the windowsill.

FLOWER: It produces white flowers, but it is very unlikely in your home.

SIZE: It can reach up to 7 feet tall in its native habitat, but in a home, it may reach 10 inches.

PROPAGATION: This may be propagated from seed.

PHILODENDRON 'MOONLIGHT'

The bright chartreuse of this plant's leaves glows in a medium- to low-light spot in the home. This self-heading philodendron does not vine, so stays a reasonable size for the home situation. The large leaves start out a bright yellow, but fade to a darker green on the older leaves at the bottom of the plant.

LIGHT PREFERENCE: A medium light ensures you will have bright yellow leaves and good growth. An east or west window would be best. If it receives too much light, the leaves will bleach out and not have the best color.

WATERING: Philodendrons like to be evenly moist, neither too wet nor too dry.

FLOWER: Philodendrons produce a finger-like spadix surrounded by a spathe, but most likely will not bloom in the home.

SIZE: They may grow up to 2 feet or more and equally that wide.

PROPAGATION: Take stem cuttings and start in a moist potting medium.

CULTIVARS: Other colors have been hybridized and include orange and variegated leaves.

- **'PRINCE OF ORANGE'**—A hybrid with dark, rust-colored new growth and medium-green older leaves.

- **'AUTUMN'**—The new growth on this plant is a dark russet color that fades to a green.

- **'PINK PRINCESS'**—A newer variety with dark burgundy leaves splashed with bright pink splotches. This plant will vine and can be grown on a pole.

PINK BUTTERFLIES

BOTANICAL NAME: *KALANCHOE DELAGOENSIS* ×
DAIGREMONTIANA 'Pink Butterflies'

This unique plant has the endearing quality of making babies on the edges of its leaves. The non-pink original form was called "mother of thousands" as its babies dropped and sprouted everywhere. The pink ones do not form roots as readily and so are not a nuisance.

LIGHT PREFERENCE: This bright-pink succulent needs plenty of light to keep its bright pink coloring. A south or west window is best.

WATERING: Plant this succulent in a fast-draining potting mix, and let it dry out a bit before watering again.

SIZE: It will grow to approximately 2 feet tall.

PROPAGATION: Take cuttings, allow them to callus, and plant in a moist potting medium.

PINK QUILL

BOTANICAL NAME: *TILLANDSIA CYANEA*

The pink bracts that produce the purple flowers are the main attraction of this bromeliad. When the flowers appear from the bract, they are small and do not last long. The pink bract, on the other hand, lasts for months. It will then turn brown and can be cut off. At this time, the parent plant will begin to fade but will be putting its last bit of energy into making offsets at its base. These can be grown to one-third to one-half the size of the parent, then cut off and potted individually, or they can be allowed to grow, eventually creating a large grouping of the plant. Quite often this plant is tossed like a poinsettia when it is done blooming.

LIGHT PREFERENCE: A medium to bright light is best, especially if you are keeping the plant and would like the new plant to bloom.

WATERING: These plants are usually grown in a potting medium, unlike most epiphytic bromeliads. Water when the medium becomes dry.

FLOWER: The small purple flowers appear from the sides of the large pink bract.

SIZE: With the bract, the plant will not be more than 10 inches tall.

PROPAGATION: This can be grown from seed, or the offsets can be removed from the parent and potted up individually.

PLUM PINE, BUDDHIST PINE, SOUTHERN YEW

BOTANICAL NAME: *PODOCARPUS MACROPHYLLUS* var. *MAKI*

In much of the United States, this plant is grown outside and is used as an evergreen hedging plant, hence, the southern yew common name. In northern climes, it is used as a houseplant. The variety **MAKI** is most often used as a houseplant, as it stays more compact with shorter leaves. It can be kept smaller with pruning or made into a shaped topiary or even a bonsai.

LIGHT PREFERENCE: This plant prefers a medium to bright light but can tolerate low light as well.

WATERING: Keep it evenly moist and plant in a fast-draining potting medium. Do not allow it to stand in water, as it is susceptible to root rot.

FLOWER: The pollen cones are white and catkin-like in shape and develop red berries. This most often will not happen in the home setting.

SIZE: The plant grows to 6 to 8 feet but with pruning can be kept 4 to 5 feet tall. It is an excellent large floor plant.

PROPAGATION: Take tip cuttings, dip in rooting hormone, and plant in moist potting medium. They can also be grown from seed.

POLKA DOT PLANT

BOTANICAL NAME: *HYPOESTES PHYLLOSTACHYA*

Polka dot plants are a smaller, endearing plant used quite often in dish gardens and terrariums. They are thin-leaved plants that need high humidity levels to grow their best. For this reason, make sure the humidity is high by using a pebble tray or placing in a terrarium.

LIGHT PREFERENCE: A medium light is best in an east window or back a few feet from a west window. If placed in an area where they get full sun exposure, the thin leaves may become washed out or even burnt.

WATERING: Keep this plant evenly moist, not allowing it to dry out, as it quite unforgiving of dry soil. Place on a pebble tray or in a terrarium to keep the humidity high. Low humidity will cause brown leaf tips and edges.

FLOWER: The flowers are small and inconspicuous.

SIZE: These may reach 16 inches or more, but can become leggy, so trim to keep it full.

PROPAGATION: Tip cuttings rooted in moist potting mix or it can be grown from seed.

PONYTAIL PALM, ELEPHANT FOOT

BOTANICAL NAME: *BEAUCARNEA RECURVATE*

The swollen caudex (stem) is the trait of this plant that is usually noticed first. The appearance of the caudex is rough and cracked and because of the shape with these traits, may suggest an elephant's foot, thus the common name. The medium green-colored fountain of strappy leaves emerging from the top of the stem give it the ponytail name. The palm part is a mystery because in no way does this resemble a palm nor is it related to them.

LIGHT PREFERENCE: Put this plant in as much light as you can. A south or west window is best.

WATERING: Plant in a fast-draining potting medium, as for cacti and other succulents. Allow the soil to dry out between waterings and if you are in doubt, don't add water, as the swollen caudex holds water.

FLOWER: With enough sun, these plants do produce a large panicle of creamy white flowers but most likely this will not occur in the home environment.

SIZE: This plant may reach 10 to 12 feet in the house but only after many years. It prefers to be in a snug pot and you will often find them in a pot just a little larger than the swollen caudex.

PROPAGATION: This plant may send up offshoots at the base of the plant, and these can be potted up individually.

POTHOS, DEVIL'S IVY

BOTANICAL NAME: *EPIPREMNUM AUREUM*

This is the ultimate houseplant and most likely you, your parents, or grandparents have had one. Your plant might even be a plant grown from a piece of theirs. It has been seen framing windows, sprawling down furniture or spanning beams on the ceiling. For a time it lost its appeal, seemingly an old-fashioned, gangly plant. Now it is back in style with many beautiful cultivars; it is an easy plant that can be kept under control with trimming. Its tolerance to low-light situations is definitely a plus in the houseplant world. These plants are often used in office settings where the only light they receive is from fluorescent lights, and they do well.

LIGHT PREFERENCE: The golden pothos that has green leaves with yellow marbling can tolerate low light such as a north window, but would prefer a medium light within a few feet of a west or east window. If your plant loses its yellow color and reverts to an all-green plant, move it into more light and it will regain its variegation.

WATERING: This plant will let you know it is dry when every leaf wilts over the edge of the pot. Yet it would be best if that never happens, as it will react by having some yellow leaves. Keep it evenly moist, but never standing in water as the roots may rot and the plant collapse, with no chance of revival.

FLOWER: This plant is grown for foliage and will not likely flower in our homes.

SIZE: In its native habitat, this vine can climb up a tree 40 to 70 feet. It may even be unrecognizable as its leaves become huge and deeply lobed. It is unlikely that will happen in our homes. The vines could become 10 to 20 feet long if left untrimmed. The leaves may only be on the ends of the otherwise-naked stems. It is better to keep your plant trimmed and full. Cut a few of the stems back to the soil line, and new sprouts will appear.

PROPAGATION: Stem cuttings can be rooted easily in water or in potting medium.

CULTIVARS:

- **'MARBLE QUEEN'**—This cultivar has white-and-green-splotched leaves that are exceptionally attractive. This cultivar will need more light as it has a lot of white on the leaves, but not full sun as those white parts will burn.

- **'N' JOY' AND 'PEARLS AND JADE'**—These cultivars are similar with more organized white-and-green patches. 'Pearls and Jade' also has small dots of green that soften the edges of the different colors. Both are newer hybrids and are exceptional.

- **'NEON'**—A bright chartreuse green cultivar that brightens any room with its yellow-green color.

- **'SILVER SATIN'**—If you have a difficult spot, this is the plant for you! The thick leaves of gray-green with silver splotches are nearly indestructible and beautiful. They are drought tolerant because of the thick leaves and also tolerant of lower light levels.

PRIMULINA

An African violet cousin, primulina was previously known under the name *CHIRITA*. The leaves of some primulinas are so decorative that if it never flowered, it wouldn't matter. However, the small trumpet-shaped flowers are an additional bonus to these charming plants.

LIGHT PREFERENCE: A medium light is preferred by primulinas, the same as their African violet cousins—because they prefer the same conditions, they could be equally happy on the same plant stand. An east window or near a west window is perfect.

WATERING: Plant in a well-drained, porous soil, keeping it evenly moist. These plants have thick succulent leaves, some more than others, and are forgiving of drying out briefly. Do not allow them to stand in water.

FLOWER: Small, up to 2-inch-long, trumpet-shaped flowers appear on stems above the foliage in colors of yellow, white, lavender, and combinations of those colors.

SIZE: There are miniature varieties as well as plants that grow to several feet across. Most offered for sale stay about the size of an African violet.

PROPAGATION: Take a single leaf cutting and place in a moist potting medium, the same as you would for an African violet. It may benefit from being covered with plastic or glass. In a few weeks, small plants will appear at the base.

CULTIVARS:

• **'VIETNAMESE VIOLET' (*PRIMULINA TAMIANA*)**—A miniature plant perfect for a terrarium. It produces tiny white flowers with a purple throat.

PURPLE HEART

BOTANICAL NAME: *SETCREASEA PALLIDA*

This plant has become popular as an annual added to combination pots in the summer, but it has been a popular houseplant for some time as well. It has purple stems to match the purple leaves, and the stems are quite succulent. It has a drooping habit and is well suited as a hanging basket.

LIGHT PREFERENCE: This plant prefers a bright light and would thrive in a south or west window.

WATERING: Keep the soil evenly moist, though the plant is somewhat forgiving of drying out, because of its succulent stems.

FLOWER: Pink flowers appear in the depression where the two leaves cross. They are not large or conspicuous, but do add a touch of color to the all-purple plant.

SIZE: It can become 8 to 12 inches tall and spread up to 20 inches.

PROPAGATION: Take tip cuttings and pot in a moist potting medium.

CULTIVARS:

There is a variegated form with light purple stripes that is worth hunting down.

PURPLE PASSION PLANT, VELVET PLANT

BOTANICAL NAME: *GYNURA AURANTIACA*

The fuzzy hairs on this plant are its most endearing feature. The bright orange flowers are also endearing, but their smell is not. These vines can be cut back to keep them compact or allowed to wander and frame a window if so desired.

LIGHT PREFERENCE: To keep its purple coloring, this plant needs bright light. If it is green, move it into more light. An east or west window would be best.

WATERING: Keep this plant evenly moist. If it is kept too wet, it will rot.

FLOWER: The flowers of the velvet plant are orange, but they have an unpleasant aroma so cutting them off while they are in bud is a good idea.

SIZE: This vining plant can become leggy. Keeping it trimmed back will make for a more attractive, bushy plant.

PROPAGATION: When you prune the vine back, use the cuttings to propagate new plants. Place them in moist potting medium and keep them reasonably moist until they root.

CULTIVARS:

- **'VARIEGATA'**—A creamy white combined with purple and green on the leaves make this a gorgeous cultivar.

QUEEN'S TEARS, FRIENDSHIP PLANT

BOTANICAL NAME: *BILLBERGIA NUTANS*

This epiphytic bromeliad is perfect for a bright window in the house. It produces flowers on long, drooping stems. This plant is most often sold growing in pots filled with coarse medium such as that used for orchids. But they would be equally happy mounted on a piece of wood. Do not fertilize these plants as it may cause the leaves to turn only green and lose their beautiful coloring. It produces plenty of offsets that are easily shared, giving it the name friendship plant.

LIGHT PREFERENCE: Give it plenty of light in the house. It needs at least a medium light to bloom.

WATERING: Pour water into the vase of leaves, letting the overflow wet the medium. Empty it often and refill with fresh water to ensure there are no stains from water additives on the leaves. Stagnant water may also lead to disease.

SIZE: They range in size from 8 to 36 inches tall, depending on the species.

PROPAGATION: Billbergias send out offsets readily, and they can be separated and potted up or mounted individually.

RADIATOR PLANT

BOTANICAL NAME: *PEPEROMIA MACULOSA*

The dark green, thick, leathery leaves make this an attractive plant. It prefers to be a bit pot-bound, so do not over-pot it.

LIGHT PREFERENCE: A medium light from an east or west window is preferred, but the low light of a north window would work as well.

WATERING: Do not overwater this plant. Its thick succulent leaves hold water. If placed in low light, less water will be needed.

FLOWER: This plant is grown for its foliage.

SIZE: The radiator plant will stay under 10 inches.

PROPAGATION: Propagate from cuttings.

ROCK FIG

BOTANICAL NAME: *FICUS PETIOLARIS*

The enlarged stem or caudex of this ornamental fig adds to the interest of the plant. The leaves are medium green with pink veins. In its natural habitat, it grows over rocks covering them with its roots—thus the name "rock fig." Any changes in its environment may cause it to drop leaves. It normally will regrow its leaves when accustomed to the new conditions. It is also used often as a bonsai plant.

LIGHT PREFERENCE: As with other members of the ficus/fig family, a high-light spot is needed. A south or west window is best.

WATERING: Keep this plant evenly moist.

FLOWER: Green flowers become small figs, but these will rarely appear in the home environment.

SIZE: In its native habitat, it may reach 20 to 30 feet tall, but by keeping it trimmed, the plant can be less than 5 feet tall in the house. It can also be kept smaller by reducing its container size, but this means you must then keep on top of the watering.

PROPAGATION: Tip cuttings can be taken and potted in a moist medium. It also can be grown from seed or air layered.

ROSARY VINE, CHAIN OF HEARTS, HEARTS ENTANGLED

BOTANICAL NAME: *CEROPEGIA WOODII*

This succulent vine, covered with speckled, heart-shaped leaves, is adorable. When the tiny purple flowers appear, it makes it all the cuter. It is well suited to a hanging basket. The small tubers that appear along the stems can be used to propagate the plant and give rise to the common name of rosary vine.

LIGHT PREFERENCE: Give this plant as much sun as you can, as otherwise the stems will elongate excessively between the leaves. Hang this plant in a south or west window.

WATERING: Water thoroughly and then allow the potting medium to dry out a bit before watering again. Never allow it to stand in water.

FLOWER: The small, under 1-inch flowers, are pinkish tubes that face upward with a dark purple top. They appear from the leaf axils.

SIZE: The plant lies quite flat to the potting mix surface, but may hang as long as 10 feet or more if there is room.

PROPAGATION: Small tubers grow along the stems and can be removed and placed on top of a moist potting medium, where they will form roots and send out stems. Tip cuttings can also be taken.

CULTIVARS:

- *CEROPEGIA WOODII* 'VARIEGATA'—This cultivar adds some pink to its white-and-green leaves, and it is gorgeous!

RUBBER PLANT

BOTANICAL NAME: *FICUS ELASTIC*

This ubiquitous houseplant staple of the 1960s is still a great houseplant where a large floor plant is needed. The large, leathery leaves make a bold statement. It is known for its adaptability to low-light situations, but would prefer a medium to bright light. If a leaf or stem is broken, a white, milky substance will appear. Stop the flow by placing a paper towel on the broken or cut end.

LIGHT PREFERENCE: A medium to bright light is best.

WATERING: Water thoroughly and then allow the potting medium to become dry an inch or two down in the pot. Too much water will cause the lower leaves to yellow and fall off.

FLOWER: This plant will not likely flower in the house.

SIZE: In its natural habitat, this plant can grow to monstrous proportions up to 100 feet tall. In the house, it may reach 10 feet or more if given the room.

PROPAGATION: Tip cuttings can be taken, dried, and potted up in a moist potting medium. It will need bottom heat to grow roots. Air layering is also an effective way of making more plants and helps if your plant has become too tall.

CULTIVARS:

• **'BURGUNDY'**—A cultivar with dark burgundy, almost-black leaves.

• **'ROBUSTA'**—A dark green variety.

• **'RUBY'**—This variegated form has medium green leaves with pink edges.

• **'TINEKE'**—Another variegated variety but with white edges.

SAGO PALM

BOTANICAL NAME: *CYCAS REVOLUTA*

This plant does have a leaf that looks like a palm and has the word "palm" in its name, but it is not related to palms but to conifers. The leaves are made up of many leaflets with sharp points that should be avoided. The petiole or stems of the leaves have barbs on them. But even with the danger factor, this is a popular plant for its strong architectural presence. It is often offered as a bonsai. When it puts out new growth, it puts out a whole ring of leaves at the same time, and this usually happens every year. This is a very slow-growing plant. This plant is extremely toxic, so keep away from pets and children.

LIGHT PREFERENCE: Bright light with full sun, such as is available in a south window, is best. When the new leaves appear, they may be elongated from insufficient light.

WATERING: Water thoroughly and then allow the medium to dry out partially before watering again.

FLOWER: Flowers do not usually appear on plants grown in the home.

SIZE: The plant can be 1 foot to 12 feet in diameter in its natural habitat, but usually less than 2 to 3 feet in the home.

PROPAGATION: Propagation is by seed or by removing the offsets from the base of the plant and potting them up individually.

SCARLET STAR

BOTANICAL NAME: *GUZMANIA LINGULATA*

This popular plant is easily found for sale, even in the grocery store. Its popularity is attributed to the beautiful colored bracts that last for many months. This bromeliad is found growing as an epiphyte on trees in the tropical rainforest, but is usually offered for sale in a container. Its leaves aren't spiny like others in the family, but soft. Used often in commercial settings, it is then discarded after the bracts fade.

LIGHT PREFERENCE: If bought with colorful bracts, this plant can be placed almost anywhere and be enjoyed for months. If you would like for offsets to be formed and grow well, keep it in a medium to bright light.

WATERING: Fill the vase formed by the leaves with water, letting it overflow into the potting medium. Water only in the leaf vase, and don't let water sit in the flower head. Like other bromeliads, the parent plant will begin to die after flowering, sending up offsets at the base of the plant.

FLOWER: The flowers are small and inconspicuous compared to the colorful bracts that surround them.

SIZE: This plant can grow approximately 2 feet tall.

PROPAGATION: The offsets that are formed by the parent plant after flowering can be separated and grown individually.

SCREW PINE

BOTANICAL NAME: *PANDANUS VEITCHII*

The screw pine is a large plant with spines along the leaves. It grows very large and would need plenty of space in a home. The variety ***PANDANUS VEITCHII***, now available to the consumer, is a beautiful yellow variegated version with multiple crowns. These are free of spines and are offered at about 18 inches high. They make a very nice foil to plain-green plants. They are relatively slow growers, and do not have the usual spiraling form of the regular screw pines.

LIGHT PREFERENCE: In the home setting, the screw pine needs to be placed in high light such as in front of a south window.

WATERING: Keep the screw pine evenly moist. It naturally grows in moist areas.

FLOWER: It most likely will not bloom in your home but does produce flowers which in turn produce fruits that resemble orange pinecones.

SIZE: These can become large trees in the wild, up to 20 feet tall or more. The newer cultivars will probably not grow taller than a few feet, and they are choice plants for displaying on a pedestal or plinth.

PROPAGATION: Propagate by offsets at the base of the plant.

SHAVING BRUSH FLOWER

BOTANICAL NAME: *HAEMANTHUS ALBIFLOS*

The bulb of this plant usually sits on top of the potting medium, adding to its interest. The leaves are rounded, and it produces two leaves at time. The flowers appear in late fall to winter and look like white shaving brushes with yellow tips. It is related to the more familiar amaryllis.

LIGHT PREFERENCE: Give the shaving brush flower a bright light but not full sun.

WATERING: Because of its water-storing bulb, the medium can be allowed to dry out quite a bit before watering again.

FLOWER: The flowers arise on short stalks and resemble an old-fashioned shaving brush. This bulb flowers better in snug quarters, so do not overpot.

SIZE: The plant grows 8 to 12 inches tall.

PROPAGATION: This plant produces offsets that can be carefully removed from the parent and potted individually.

SHOOTING STAR HOYA

BOTANICAL NAME: *HOYA MULTIFLORA*

Unlike many other hoyas, the shooting star is not a succulent. The leaves are thin and dark green. It does have pendulous stems and makes for a great hanging basket. The beautiful white-and-yellow flowers that resemble shooting stars may appear more than once in the year. This is an easy plant to grow and bloom.

LIGHT PREFERENCE: Bright light is needed to form flowers. A south or west window is best.

WATERING: Because this isn't a succulent, it will need more water than its other family members. Plant in a well-drained potting medium and keep it evenly moist.

FLOWER: The clusters of white flowers resemble small shooting stars with yellow tails. As with most flowers of the hoya family, the nectar is excessive and drips off the tips of the flowers. With that in mind, place your plant where it won't drip on furniture or rugs.

SIZE: The stems may reach 4 to 5 feet, but they can be trimmed to keep the plant smaller.

PROPAGATION: Propagate from tip cuttings in moist potting medium.

SHRIMP PLANT

BOTANICAL NAME: *JUSTICIA BRANDEGEANA*

The bracts (or modified leaves) are slightly curved and shaped like shrimp; small white flowers peek out from between the bracts. The flowers are sometimes overlooked because the bracts are so showy. Even the color of the bracts reminds one of shrimp. This is an easy houseplant with unique characteristics.

LIGHT PREFERENCE: These plants need a medium to bright light to ensure the blooms are formed.

WATERING: Keep the potting medium evenly moist. If the medium is kept too wet or too dry, it may drop its leaves.

FLOWER: The flowers are small white tubes that peek out of the colored bracts, which are a peachy-red color.

SIZE: In your home, the shrimp plant may be 1 to 3 feet tall. It can get leggy, so keep it trimmed to keep it compact.

PROPAGATION: Tip cuttings can be rooted in a moist potting medium.

CULTIVARS:

• **'YELLOW QUEEN'**—Yellow bracts surround the white flowers.

• **'VARIEGATA'**—This variety has the shrimp-colored flowers, and the foliage is variegated white and green.

SILVER SPRINKLES

BOTANICAL NAME: *PILEA GLAUCA*

This diminutive, low-growing plant is a nice groundcover. The small red stems hold up small silver leaves less than ¼ inch wide. It is a perfect terrarium or dish garden groundcover.

LIGHT PREFERENCE: This plant does need a medium light to stay compact and a bright light if it is growing in a terrarium.

WATERING: Keep it evenly moist. If left to get too dry, it will drop its leaves. It will do well in the humid environment of a terrarium if in enough light.

FLOWER: Tiny flower clusters rise a few inches above the foliage, but may not be seen in the home environment.

SIZE: This groundcover is 2 to 4 inches tall.

PROPAGATION: This spreading plant could be split apart and potted separately, or take tip cuttings and root in a moist medium.

SILVER SQUILL

BOTANICAL NAME: *LEDEBOURIA SOCIALIS* (syn. *SCILLA VIOLACEA*)

This small, bulbous plant has beautiful strappy leaves mottled with splotches of dark green. The underside of the leaf is a burgundy color. The bulb is usually sitting on top of the medium, adding to the uniqueness of this plant.

LIGHT PREFERENCE: Give the silver squill a bright light such as a south or west window. If light isn't bright enough, the leaves will stretch toward the light.

WATERING: Water thoroughly and then let the soil dry out partially before watering again. Because the bulbs above the medium store moisture, they can take a bit of dryness. Yet, if it is allowed to dry too much, the plant will lose leaves.

FLOWER: The tiny flowers are on stems that rise above the foliage an inch or two. Each flower is pink, green, and white, and quite beautiful; unfortunately, they are very small. When they bloom, find a magnifying glass and look at them closely.

SIZE: This plant stays under 10 inches tall.

PROPAGATION: The plant multiplies rapidly and is easily pulled apart. They look better with a few pieces in one pot, instead of individually potted.

SILVER TREE

BOTANICAL NAME: *PILEA SPRUCEANA*

The bronze-and-silver leaves of this small houseplant are a welcome relief from an all-green palette. It is an easy-to-grow houseplant and is also suitable for a terrarium or miniature garden.

LIGHT PREFERENCE: A medium light is perfect for this plant, such as an east window.

WATERING: Water thoroughly and then again when the top 1 to 2 inches of medium is dry. Err on the dry side for this plant, rather than keeping it too moist.

FLOWER: Flowers are inconspicuous.

SIZE: This is a smaller houseplant at 6 to 12 inches.

PROPAGATION: Take tip cuttings and pot in a moist potting medium.

SLIPPER ORCHID

BOTANICAL NAME: *PAPHIOPEDILUM*

This orchid is easy to grow and good for beginner orchid growers. The flowers of the slipper orchid are so gorgeous and exotic looking, they may intimidate some from attempting to grow them. Fear not: they are quite easy and need care not unlike that of African violets. They may have marbled or mottled as well as solid-green leaves. Phaphiopedilum having silver-mottled leaves are better suited to warm house temperatures than those having plain-green leaves that need cooler temperatures. The foliage makes it beautiful even when the plant isn't flowering. Most are terrestrial, meaning they grow in organic matter as opposed to being epiphytic, or growing in trees.

LIGHT PREFERENCE: These orchids are considered low-light orchids in their native habitat, but will not bloom in a low-light area in our homes. A medium light, such as an east window, would be best for the flowering success of the plant, or grow it under electric lights.

WATERING: As with other orchids, watering practices depend on the medium the plant is growing in, temperature, and light levels. If growing in moss, wait until the moss has turned a lighter color at the surface. If growing in a finely chopped fir bark, then water when the color of the bark is not as dark as it was when first watered. They need to be watered regularly as they have no means of storing water, unlike some orchids.

FLOWER: The flowers have a pouch on the front of the flower, giving it the look of a slipper and its common name. The flowers can last many weeks and come in many combinations of colors.

SIZE: The leaves rarely are higher than 6 inches and may be up to a 1 inch wide. The flowers rise up above the foliage 10 to 12 inches.

PROPAGATION: The plant will make offsets, and these can be divided and potted up separately.

SNAKE PLANT, BOW STRING HEMP PLANT, MOTHER-IN-LAW'S TONGUE

BOTANICAL NAME: *SANSEVIERIA TRIFASCIATA*

The snake plant family has certainly received a bad reputation as boring, ho-hum plants. Yet grown well, they can be a beautiful plant with many forms and cultivars available. Previously placed in dark corners and allowed to languish, they have come into their own as air purifiers. This quality along with better information about growing this plant has given it the place in the houseplant world it deserves. It is tall, up to 4 feet, and has green leaves with darker green markings.

LIGHT PREFERENCE: The snake plant will tolerate low-light situations but will thrive in a medium to bright light.

WATERING: Many a snake plant has been killed by overwatering. If they are in a low-light situation, water infrequently, letting the medium become quite dry before watering again. If in a high light, they will use more water. Never allow a sansevieria to stand in water. Rotten snake plants are slimy and smell horrible!

FLOWER: If given enough light, a stem will appear from the plant and aromatic white flowers will follow.

SIZE: These plants can be a few inches tall to many feet tall. There are many cultivars available.

PROPAGATION: Because of the multiple crowns this plant produces, separating is the simplest way to propagate them. Leaves cut into 2- to 3-inch sections and planted upright will form new plants at the base. Make sure the sections are planted with the top side up or they will not grow.

CULTIVARS:

- **'FERNWOOD'** —This is a newer variety, resembling a small cylindrica form, but its leaves are not completely round. Its mottled foliage is attractive. Under 2 feet.

- **S. CYLINDRICA**—Instead of flat leaves, this plant's leaves are round and very sharply pointed. It can grow to over 6 feet.

- **'BANTEL'S SENSATION'**—The bright white-and-green-striped leaves of this cultivar are very striking. It will be 3 to 4 feet tall.

- **'TWISTER'**—Its undulating, twisting leaves make this an interesting specimen. It will grow up to 12 inches tall.

- **'GOLD FLAME'**—It has bright yellow leaves with dark green stripes.

- **'LAURENTII'**—This green-striped variety with yellow edges is a very popular old cultivar, growing 3 to 4 feet tall.

- **'MASON'S CONGO' (S. MASONIANA)**—The leaves of this large variety can be 8 to 10 inches wide and the plant can grow 3 to 4 feet tall.

SNOW BUSH

BOTANICAL NAME: *BREYNIA DISTICHA ROSEO-PICTA*

The highly variegated leaves of this plant are mottled with white-and-pink splotches; the pink color is most concentrated in the tips of the branches, making it seem as if they have flowers. The white variegation gives the effect that snow has fallen on the plant, hence the common name. The stems are a reddish color and wiry. It needs to be kept well-watered or the small leaves will fall off. Keep the tips pinched to keep the plant compact.

LIGHT PREFERENCE: Give this plant a bright light to keep the color at its best and to promote flowering.

WATERING: Keep it evenly moist, never letting it completely dry out, or the leaves will fall off. Keep the humidity up by placing the plant on a pebble tray.

FLOWER: The flowers are little green bells that hang down from the underside of the stems. They are almost impossible to detect but are fascinating if you notice them.

SIZE: This plant may get 1 to 3 feet tall and wide.

PROPAGATION: Take tip cuttings and root in moist potting medium with bottom heat and cover to keep humidity high.

SPIDER PLANT, AIRPLANE PLANT

BOTANICAL NAME: *CHLOROPHYTUM COMOSUM*

The much-loved spider plant is one of the most popular houseplants grown. The variegated version is usually the one offered for sale and most often in a hanging basket. The miniature plants floating in the air attached to long stems from the parent are the most endearing characteristic of this plant. The tuberous root system means it will need to be up-potted or divided when the roots fill the pot or it may break the container.

LIGHT PREFERENCE: The solid-green version of this plant could take low light but the variegated versions would need a medium to bright light.

WATERING: Keep the spider plant evenly moist. Brown tips appear due to salt buildup from fertilizing the plant. Flush the plant often to rectify the problem, and trim the leaves to remove the brown tips.

FLOWER: Small, star-shaped, white flowers appear in conjunction with the small plants at the end of the stems. They are not extremely showy, but are delicate and pretty.

SIZE: The plants are 1 to 2 feet tall, but the stems cascade 2 to 3 feet over the edge of the container.

PROPAGATION: The little plantlets at the ends of the stems can be removed and rooted in a moist potting medium. To ensure faster rooting, leave the babies attached to the parent plant and pin them to a container of moist medium. When they are well rooted, cut them away from the parent. You can also divide a large plant into smaller pieces and pot each individually.

CULTIVAR:

• **'BONNIE'**—This cultivar has curly leaves.

STICKS ON FIRE, PENCIL CACTUS

BOTANICAL NAME: *EUPHORBIA TIRUCALLI*

The all-green version of this succulent plant is called "pencil cactus" as its stems are approximately the size and shape of pencils. The cactus part is a mystery as it is a succulent member of the spurge family with no spines at all. The newer variety has been hybridized to have red ends and so has the name "sticks on fire." It has become popular to use this plant as the "thriller" in the center of full sun combination pots. Without the bright light or full sun it would receive outside, the red tips may not "burn" in our homes, but it is a unique plant to grow on a bright windowsill. Be careful when handling as its white sap is irritating.

LIGHT PREFERENCE: Give these succulents as much light as possible, especially with the red variety or otherwise it will turn green.

WATERING: Plant in a fast-draining potting medium, allowing it to become quite dry between waterings.

FLOWER: This plant will most likely not flower in the house.

SIZE: In its natural habitat, it could grow to a 30-foot-tall shrub, but in your home may reach the ceiling. It can be trimmed to keep it smaller.

PROPAGATION: Remove a segment of the plant, allow it to callus over, then place it in a moist medium to root.

STRIPED INCH PLANT

BOTANICAL NAME: *CALLISIA ELEGANS*

This is a creeping plant than can quickly cover a large area, making it perfect for a hanging basket. The medium-green leaves are covered with delicate white lines. It can become lanky, so keep it trimmed and use the cuttings for new plants.

LIGHT PREFERENCE: A medium to bright light is best.

WATERING: Keep it evenly moist.

FLOWER: Tiny white flowers appear with enough light.

SIZE: This vine rarely grows higher than 6 inches but spreads much further.

PROPAGATION: It is easily propagated by stem cuttings placed in moist potting medium.

SWISS CHEESE PLANT, FRUIT SALAD PLANT

BOTANICAL NAME: *MONSTERA DELICIOSA*

This large plant, like the rubber plant, was a staple of the mid-century decorating scheme. The high ceilings and open-concept floor plan that is popular today has brought this large plant back with a vengeance. It is now one of the most popular plants for its large architectural presence and ease of care. The large, perforated, lobed leaves are unique: They are thought to have holes in the leaves to combat the strong winds and large amounts of rain they can be exposed to high in the trees of the rainforest. They do send out aerial roots to gather more moisture and to stabilize themselves. Do not allow them to attach themselves to your wood floors or other surfaces as they will leave marks when pulled away.

LIGHT PREFERENCE: Monstera can tolerate low light, but would prefer a medium to bright light. In their native habitat, they start life on the jungle floor and scramble along until they find a tree to cling to, then climb to the top for light.

WATERING: Keep this plant evenly moist, letting it get quite dry before watering again.

FLOWER: The flower most likely will not appear in the house. It gets its name "fruit salad" because the ripe fruit—which resembles an ear of corn—is edible and said to taste like a cross between banana and pineapple. The unripe fruit is not edible and may cause irritation to the mouth and throat.

SIZE: This plant can get quite large and will need a lot of room to grow. Growing it on a moss pole is best so it has something to cling to. It may reach 10 feet or taller.

PROPAGATION: Propagate by stem tip cuttings potted in moist potting medium. It can also be air layered.

CULTIVAR:

- **'VARIEGATA'**—A variegated form that has splotches of light green and white on the dark green leaves.

SWISS CHEESE VINE

BOTANICAL NAME: *MONSTERA FRIEDRICHSTHALII* (syn. *MONSTERA ADANSONII*)

This plant shares its name with the Swiss cheese plant but is a much smaller vine and has leaves with solid edges and the leaf itself is filled with perforations. It's a good alternative to the extremely large *DELICIOSA* and yet has similar unique leaves.

LIGHT PREFERENCE: This plant will take a low light, but would prefer a medium to bright light.

WATERING: Water thoroughly and then let it dry a bit, but not completely, before watering again.

FLOWER: It will most likely will not flower in the home.

SIZE: This vining plant would like to have a moss pole to climb and will reach up to 6 feet.

PROPAGATION: Stem cuttings can be potted in a moist potting medium.

TEDDY BEAR PLANT, PANDA PLANT

BOTANICAL NAME: *KALANCHOE TOMENTOSA*

This fuzzy succulent is loved by children and adults alike. Children like to pet the leaves, which are mostly covered with silver fuzz with brown accents on their edges.

LIGHT PREFERENCE: Give this succulent as much sun as possible. A south or west windowsill would be best.

WATERING: This succulent needs a well-drained potting medium. Let it dry down a bit before watering again.

FLOWER: It is unlikely the yellow-green flowers will appear in the home setting.

SIZE: It can grow 1 to 3 feet tall.

PROPAGATION: Leaf cuttings should be allowed to callus over before planting in a moist potting soil.

CULTIVAR:

- **'CHOCOLATE SOLDIER'**—Instead of having small rust-colored markings on the edges of the leaves, the whole leaf is rust colored.

TRADESCANTIA

BOTANICAL NAME: *TRADESCANTIA ZEBRINA*

This vine is a popular hanging basket plant. The attractive, iridescent, striped leaves shimmer in the light. It's an easy-to-grow plant and is often used outside in the summer. It is not easily moved inside from outside, however, so take cuttings and start over instead for best results.

LIGHT PREFERENCE: This plant does best in a medium to bright light. An east or west window works well.

WATERING: Keep the potting medium evenly moist, but not too wet. If it is too wet, stem and root rot can set in. Because the stems are succulent, it is forgiving of drying out temporarily.

FLOWER: The lavender flowers are tiny and three-petaled, but they rarely bloom indoors.

SIZE: This vine typically doesn't grow taller than 6 inches, but can trail 2 feet long and more.

PROPAGATION: Take stem cuttings and root in a moist potting medium.

TRAILING WATERMELON BEGONIA, RAINBOW VINE

BOTANICAL NAME: *PELLIONIA REPENS*

The dark burgundy edges and marbled middle give the appearance of a watermelon rind, giving this plant its common name. It's a low-growing vine that is perfect for a terrarium if the light is bright enough.

LIGHT PREFERENCE: To keep the rich burgundy color of the leaves, give this plant a medium to bright light. An east or west window is perfect.

WATERING: Keep this plant evenly moist to prevent leaf drop.

FLOWER: Small white clusters of flowers rise above the foliage a couple of inches. They are not showy.

SIZE: This mat-forming plant rarely exceeds 2 to 3 inches tall, but can trail up to a foot.

PROPAGATION: Tip cuttings are easily rooted in a moist potting medium.

TREE PHILODENDRON

BOTANICAL NAME: *PHILODENDRON SELLOUM* (syn. *PHILODENDRON BIPINNATIFIDUM*)

This is another architectural plant popular for a large room setting. The leaves can be up to 4 feet long. It's an easy plant to grow as long as it isn't overwatered. It tolerates low light but would do better in a medium to bright light.

LIGHT PREFERENCE: These large plants can tolerate a low-light situation but would prefer a medium light such as in an east or west window.

WATERING: Keep the potting medium evenly moist.

FLOWER: The white flowers probably will not appear in the home setting.

SIZE: This plant could reach proportions of up to 10 feet wide and tall, but may not achieve that size in the house.

PROPAGATION: Propagate by taking tip cuttings and rooting in a moist potting medium.

UMBRELLA TREE

BOTANICAL NAME: *SCHEFFLERA ACTINOPHYLLA*

The umbrella tree is a large plant with palmate leaves that can reach a foot or more across. If you have a large room with bright light, this is the plant for you. It is quite easy to grow and makes quite a statement.

LIGHT PREFERENCE: Keep your plant in a medium to bright spot, especially if it's the variegated version, to keep the color bright. If it starts to get leggy, move it into a brighter light.

WATERING: Keep this plant evenly moist, never letting it dry out. Occasionally take it to the shower if possible and spray it down to keep it clean. Otherwise, it is difficult to wash each individual leaf. Do not let it stand in water as the results will be yellow, dropping leaves.

FLOWER: The bright red spikes of flowers will not appear in the home setting.

SIZE: In its natural habitat, these trees can reach up to 40 feet tall. In your home, it can be kept under 10 feet with pruning.

PROPAGATION: Take cuttings of the stem tips and pot in a moist potting medium.

CULTIVARS:

- **'AMATE'**—This cultivar has been bred for better disease and insect resistance for the interior plant industry. It also does better in low-light conditions.

- **'AMATE SOLEIL'**—This variety has a vivid chartreuse color and brightens up any interior.

VARIEGATED SABER FIG, BANANA LEAF FIG

BOTANICAL NAME: *FICUS MACLELLANDII* 'Alii Variegated'

The strappy leaf version of the weeping fig is much easier to grow than the regular weeping fig. It does not drop leaves when it is stressed, such as being moved across the room. The bright chartreuse color of the leaves with dark green splotches in their middles adds a bright spot to any room. The plain-green version would be easier to locate for purchase and is usually found as a tree-form standard. It also can take a lower light level, as it has no variegation.

LIGHT PREFERENCE: This plant needs a medium to bright light. The bright light will keep the color of the plant vibrant.

WATERING: Keep this plant evenly moist, not standing in water. If the plant dries out, some leaves may drop.

FLOWER: It is unlikely to bloom in the home.

SIZE: This plant could grow up to 10 or more feet.

PROPAGATION: It can be propagated from cuttings, but may take a couple of months. Air layering can also be used.

VARIEGATED STROMANTHE

BOTANICAL NAME: *STROMANTHE SANGUINEA* 'Triostar'

The variegated green-and-white leaves with burgundy undersides of this plant are stunning. At night, they fold up like a prayer plant, a relative in the Marantaceae family. This plant is quite often used outside in the summer in mixed combination pots for shady situations. The white parts of the leaves will burn in full sun. In the house, though, it will need a bright light to keep its colors.

LIGHT PREFERENCE: Keep this plant in bright light to keep the colors of its foliage bright. A western exposure would be best.

WATERING: Keep this plant evenly moist, never dry, but not standing in water. They definitely need high humidity, so stand the pot on a pebble tray.

FLOWER: The reddish flowers are held above the foliage, but most likely won't occur in the home.

SIZE: It can reach 2 to 3 feet tall and 1 to 2 feet wide.

PROPAGATION: This plant naturally forms clumps, so divide the plant and pot up divisions individually.

VARIEGATED WAX VINE, WAX FLOWER

BOTANICAL NAME: *HOYA CARNOSA* 'Tricolor'

The hoya flowers, when they appear, are gorgeous and look unreal, thus the wax flower name. The green leaves have white-and-pink edges. They are easily found to purchase and easy to grow.

LIGHT PREFERENCE: If you would like to see the gorgeous pink flowers, this succulent vine will need a bright light such as a south or west window. This plant does not like to be cold, so keep it in a warm spot. In the lower light levels in the winter, wait longer between waterings.

WATERING: This is a succulent vine and so would like to be watered thoroughly and then allowed to dry a bit before watering again. If the leaves begin to wrinkle, it has become too dry. In the lower light levels in the winter, wait longer between waterings. Do not allow it to stand in water.

FLOWER: The pink flowers are clustered in a half-ball shapes, like an upside-down umbrella. The flowers are baby pink with burgundy centers. When they flower, do not trim off the spur the flower came from, as it will flower in the same place again.

SIZE: This vine can get quite long and, if not in a hanging container, it could be trained on a trellis or as a wreath shape.

PROPAGATION: Take stem cuttings and root in a moist potting medium.

VELDT GRAPE

BOTANICAL NAME: *CISSUS QUADRANGULARIS*

This unusual plant has four-sided stems which grow as long as they are allowed. It is often grown in a hanging basket. Its succulent stems grow in segments that can be easily separated and propagated. It is a plant that looks like no other: in the grape family, it grows leaves that resemble tiny grape leaves where the segments meet.

LIGHT PREFERENCE: Give this plant a bright light.

WATERING: This succulent can be allowed to become quite dry between waterings. If it is kept well-watered, it will have tiny grape-like leaves.

FLOWER: It does flower but most likely not in the home.

SIZE: These many stemmed plants can grow as long as allowed.

PROPAGATION: Separate the segments, let them callus over, and plant them in a moist potting medium.

WATERMELON PEPEROMIA

WATERMELON VINE

BOTANICAL NAME: *PEPEROMIA ARGYREIA*

Once you've seen this plant, the common name will make perfect sense. It looks just like the rind of a watermelon. The silver leaves have green stripes and a teardrop shape with red stems. These small, colorful plants are easy to grow as long as they don't become waterlogged.

LIGHT PREFERENCE: Give them a medium to bright light such as an east or west window.

WATERING: Keep the potting medium evenly moist but not wet, as the plants easily rot. Let the medium dry down a bit before watering again.

FLOWER: The slim stalks rise above the foliage and look like little greenish mouse tails. They are inconspicuous.

SIZE: It will grow 6 to 12 inches tall.

PROPAGATION: This plant can be propagated from a leaf cutting like an African violet. Place in a moist potting medium and cover with plastic or glass but watch the humidity levels so that the leaf doesn't rot. Small plants will appear at the base of the leaf.

BOTANICAL NAME: *PELLIONIA PULCHRA*

The watermelon vine has veining on its leaves that resembles a watermelon rind, and to top it off, it has reddish stems. It is quite often used in terrariums and vivariums. It is usually sold as either a small plant for a terrarium or as a large plant in a hanging basket. This is an easy vine to grow. Though called a vine, it is more of a trailing plant.

LIGHT PREFERENCE: This vine needs only a low to medium light to be happy.

WATERING: It appreciates an evenly moist potting medium. If it becomes too dry, it will lose its older leaves. It does not want to stand in water, either.

FLOWER: Small clusters of tiny cream flowers rise on stems about 2 inches above the foliage. They are not showy and may not be noticed.

SIZE: The plant is only a couple of inches high and spreads or hangs down from the container about 1 foot. If it gets leggy, pinch the ends off and use them to make more.

PROPAGATION: Take tip cuttings and root them in a moist potting medium.

WEEPING FIG

BOTANICAL NAME: *FICUS BENJAMINA*

This popular plant graces many mall plantings and can become large and stately in large inside spaces. These trees can become large in their natural habitat, up to 50 feet tall and could become a tall tree in your home, but trimming it will keep it a reasonable size. They are known for dropping leaves but only do this when their environment changes. Once it acclimates to the changes, it will settle in and grow nicely. This tree has small leaves, so even though it is a large tree, it provides a softer look instead of an architectural statement. Find one with a braided stem for added interest.

LIGHT PREFERENCE: Although this plant can live in low-light situations, it will be fuller and grow better in a bright light, even full sun.

WATERING: Keep this plant evenly watered. Remember, changes in growing situations will cause it to drop leaves. Drying out and overwatering will trigger this, so try to keep it evenly moist.

FLOWER: It rarely flowers indoors.

SIZE: This plant is normally in the 2 to 10 feet range indoors.

PROPAGATION: Tip cuttings may root in a moist medium, or the plant can be air layered.

CULTIVARS:

- **'NEON MARGUERITE'**—A variety with darker green blotches on bright chartreuse leaves. The older leaves turn to a darker green.

- **'STARLIGHT'**—A beautiful green variety with lots of white variegation.

YUCCA CANE

BOTANICAL NAME: *YUCCA GUATEMALENSIS* (syn. *YUCCA ELEPHANTIPES*)

The plants have a coarse texture and are usually offered for sale in containers with three sizes of canes, to make for a fuller, more attractive plant. The bold look adds to a modern home setting and is gaining in popularity. Its relative ease of care adds to its popularity.

LIGHT PREFERENCE: Give this plant as much sun as you can. A south-facing window with plenty of sun would be best for this plant. It may do okay in lower light levels but quite often the leaves will flop, losing their upright look.

WATERING: Water thoroughly and then allow the potting medium to dry down quite a bit before watering again. Plant in a fast-draining potting medium. Never leave it standing in water or keep it overly wet.

FLOWER: White flowers are produced in the wild, but most likely not in the home.

SIZE: Although this plant can become large in its natural habitat, in the home situation, 6 to 7 feet is the height to expect.

PROPAGATION: Cut a shoot off the cane, let it callus over, and then plant in a moist potting medium. The canes can be cut into pieces, allowed to dry, and planted in a moist potting medium.

ZZ PLANT

BOTANICAL NAME: *ZAMIOCULCAS ZAMIIFOLIA*

This has become one of the most popular houseplants in the past few years as it can take low light and still look amazing. This plant has shiny, dark green leaves with a strong architectural appearance. The leaves are upright and are made up of many leaflets on each rachis (stem of a compound leaf), the actual "stem" being the underground tuberous rhizomes. The unusual part of this plant is that it can grow new plants from an individual leaflet, but it takes quite a long time.

LIGHT PREFERENCE: While it is true this plant can tolerate low light levels for quite some time, it would prefer a medium to bright light to grow well.

WATERING: This plant has been touted as extremely drought tolerant, and whereas it can take long periods between waterings, this depends on the level of light it is growing in. If it dries down too much, it will drop leaflets.

FLOWER: The flower may appear, consisting of a white spadix surrounded by a white spathe. This may not happen in the home, but as this plant is grown for its beautiful foliage, the flowers would be an added bonus.

SIZE: This plant can reach up to 3 feet tall.

PROPAGATION: As mentioned before, this plant can be propagated from one leaflet. Place the cut end into moist potting medium and cover with plastic or glass. This process may take many months. The plant can also be divided.

MODERATELY
EASY TO GROW

---

*This group of plants will need a little more care
than the group of plants previously discussed.
They may not be harder to care for, but need
more time and careful attention. If you have
the extra time to devote to your plants, then
these are for you.*

AFRICAN VIOLET

BOTANICAL NAME: *SAINTPAULIA*

African violets have received a bad rap as a grandma plant. Maybe your grandma did raise them, but they have come a long way since then. The number of colors, sizes, and leaf variations is mind boggling. They have been hybridized to have yellow flowers, chimera flowers and leaves, and so much more. Give this "grandma plant" another look.

LIGHT PREFERENCE: An east or west window is the best for African violets. Growing them under electric lights for 12 hours a day helps with symmetry and flowering.

WATERING: Keep your African violet evenly moist. Wick watering is a popular way to keep violets moist at all times. If your violet dries out and the growing medium pulls away from the sides of the pot, immerse it in water to rehydrate the medium.

FLOWER: Flowers range from yellow to purple with red, pink, green, and white in between. There are single, double, and semi-double flower types.

SIZE: There are standard, semi-miniature, and miniature plants. These range in size from 3 inches to 16 inches in diameter. Since the African Violet Society of America formed in 1946, the hybridizing of African violets has created more hybrids than can be kept track of.

PROPAGATION: The easiest way to propagate African violets is to simply cut a leaf off and pot it up in a potting media. Leave a 1-inch stem on the leaf and insert it at a 45-degree angle into the medium, making sure to keep the medium moist. In 6 to 8 weeks, baby plants should be ready to be removed and planted separately in their own pots.

ARTILLERY PLANT

BOTANICAL NAME: *PILEA MICROPHYLLA*

The fine texture of this plant gives it a ferny appearance. The name comes from the way the plant ejects pollen from its small flowers. The diminutive size of the leaves and the plant make it a perfect fairy garden addition. Pinch it back to keep it bushy and smaller.

LIGHT PREFERENCE: A medium light is best, such as in an east or west window.

WATERING: Keep evenly moist, watering when the top of the potting medium feels dry. Do not keep it overly wet, as it easily rots.

FLOWER: Tiny greenish flowers are inconspicuous.

SIZE: This grows 8 to 12 inches tall.

PROPAGATION: Propagate from stem cuttings potted in moist medium.

CULTIVAR:

• **'VARIEGATA'**—A cultivar with green, white, and pink leaves.

BABY'S TEARS, MIND-YOUR-OWN-BUSINESS

BOTANICAL NAME: *SOLEIROLIA SOLEIROLII*

This is a creeping plant that will cover the container it is growing in and spill over the rim. It needs a potting medium to live on, so won't go too far down the container. This plant loves moisture and humidity so it makes a great terrarium plant. It can be used to cover a stuffed topiary frame as long as it is kept well-watered.

LIGHT PREFERENCE: It will grow in low light but prefers a medium light. An east or west window would be perfect.

WATERING: This plant prefers to be on the moist side at all times. Do not let it dry out. Raise the humidity as well by placing it on a pebble tray.

FLOWER: It may produce tiny white flowers if it has enough light.

SIZE: This plant grows close to the medium level so it can be a few inches high, but it spreads only as far as the container will allow it to.

PROPAGATION: Divide the plant into smaller clumps and pot individually.

BEEFSTEAK BEGONIA

BOTANICAL NAME: *BEGONIA ERYTHROPHYLLA*

The beefsteak begonia is a plant your grandparents may have had. It is an older variety, but beautiful. This is an example of a rhizomatous begonia and it, like others in that group, have thick, succulent stems that grow over the soil surface, sending out foliage on the top of the stem and roots on the bottom. This particular begonia has large round leaves that are dark green with a burgundy underside; they resemble large lily pads. In the winter, they will send up a spray of delicate flowers.

LIGHT PREFERENCE: This begonia can grow in a north window but may not bloom and would prefer an eastern exposure.

WATERING: Water the begonia thoroughly, never allowing it to stand in water. Then let it dry out a bit before watering again. Err on the dry side with this plant to avoid rotting. Use a well-drained potting medium.

FLOWER: In the wintertime, sprays of delicate flowers are on stems above the plant. They can be a light pink to white.

SIZE: This can become quite a sizeable begonia, at least 2 feet tall and 2 to 3 feet wide.

PROPAGATION: Take cuttings of the succulent stem and pin the sections to a moist medium.

Not a cultivar of the beefsteak, but another rhizomatous begonia is 'Madame Queen.' It displays the same dark green leaf with burgundy undersides, but has an extremely ruffled edge that displays the burgundy underside on the top edge of the leaf.

BIRD'S NEST FERN

BOTANICAL NAME: *ASPLENIUM NIDUS*

This bright green fern probably does not resemble the picture you have in your mind of a typical fern. The fronds are an entire leaf, with no leaflets on the frond. Instead, the fronds of this fern form a bowl shape that has a "nest" made from a brown fuzzy substance from which arise the new fronds. As the fronds form, the round shape of the unfurling fronds look like small "eggs" in the "nest." It's a beautiful fern with an unusual shape.

LIGHT PREFERENCE: Place this fern in a medium light: an east window would be best, but they will grow in a north window as well.

WATERING: Keep this fern evenly moist, never allowing it dry out completely. Keep it out of standing water and raise the humidity by setting it on a pebble tray. Water around the edge of the pot, never in the center of the "nest" as it may rot the plant.

FLOWER: Ferns do not produce flowers.

SIZE: These ferns get quite large in their native habitats and can grow 4 feet high and 3 feet wide in your home if the conditions are favorable.

PROPAGATION: Spores that appear on the back of the fronds can be sown.

CULTIVARS:

- **'VICTORIA'**—A cultivar that has thinner leaves with wavy edges like a fluted pie crust.

- **'CRISPY WAVE'**—This cultivar has leaves that are entirely wavy, not just along the edges like the 'Victoria'.

BOSTON FERN

BOTANICAL NAME: *NEPHROLEPIS EXALTATA* 'Bostoniensis'

This popular fern is an easy houseplant as long as you can provide it with good light and plenty of humidity. Many admire this fern, grow it outside all summer, and yet when they bring it in the house, are disappointed when it drops leaflets like crazy. This is normal, especially as it acclimates from the light levels and humidity outside to the lower levels in our dry, dark homes. Acclimating the fern to lower light levels before bringing it inside will help reduce the number of leaflets dropped. Yet even one that has always been a houseplant is going to drop some leaflets in its normal aging process. This is a beautiful airy plant and worth a little clean up. Place it on a pedestal to show off its airy, arching fronds.

LIGHT PREFERENCE: Ferns in general love a medium light. They can tolerate low light such as a north window provides, though the medium light in an east window would be its preference.

WATERING: Keep this fern evenly moist, never allowing it to dry out. Use a potting medium with plenty of peat, yet with good drainage. Place on a pebble tray to raise the humidity.

FLOWER: Ferns do not produce flowers.

SIZE: This is a large fern that can become 3 feet tall and wide.

PROPAGATION: This fern can be divided and potted up individually. It may also be propagated from the long runners it sends out. Pin them to a container of moist potting medium while still attached to the parent. With time, a new plant will form.

CULTIVARS:

• **COTTON CANDY FERN (***NEPHROLEPIS EXALTATA* **'SUZY WONG')** —A fluffy, foamy fern that does resemble swirls of cotton candy. This is a newer variety that also needs plenty of water and humidity.

• **LEMON BUTTON FERN (***N. EXALTATA* **'LEMON BUTTON')**—The leaflets of this diminutive fern are round like buttons and are staggered up the frond, overlapping each other. This cultivar also needs moisture and humidity.

• **RITA'S GOLD FERN (***N. EXALTATA* **'RITA'S GOLD')** —This bright chartreuse fern was discovered by Rita Randolph and, after giving a piece to Alan Armitage, it was trialed and he named it 'Rita's Gold'. An exceptional variety that adds a bright spot to any room. It is also used extensively in shady combination containers outside.

• **'TIGER FERN' (***N. EXALTATA***)**—A cultivar with striking variegation on the fronds.

BRAKE FERN, SILVER RIBBON FERN, TABLE FERN

BOTANICAL NAME: *PTERIS CRETICA* 'Albolineata'

This is a unique fern that has fronds with one to five pairs of pinnae (the primary division of a fern frond) that look more like ribbons than the leaflets normally seen on ferns. This cultivar has a white stripe running down the center of the light green fronds. It mixes well with other ferns as it has such a different look.

LIGHT PREFERENCE: A medium to bright light is best, such as an east window or set back a bit from a west window. It really would not like to be in a north window and may lose some of its variegation in the lower light.

WATERING: As with most ferns, keep it evenly moist, never allowing it to dry out or stand in water. Raise the humidity by placing it on a pebble tray.

FLOWER: Ferns do not flower.

SIZE: This is a smaller fern and grows 1 to 2 feet tall and wide.

PROPAGATION: The plant may be divided to propagate.

RELATED FERN:

• **TOOTHBRAKE FERN (*PTERIS DENTATA STRAMINEA*)** —This fern needs the same conditions as listed above.

BUTTERFLY PALM, ARECA PALM

BOTANICAL NAME: *DYPSIS LUTESCENS*

This palm is bright green with yellow stems. It's easy to grow, as long as it isn't overwatered, and is one of the top air-cleaning plants. Place it in a prominent spot because it is a beautiful focal plant for any room.

LIGHT PREFERENCE: A bright light is best, but without direct sun.

WATERING: Water thoroughly and then allow the top of the potting medium to dry slightly before watering again. Use a well-drained potting medium, never allowing the palm to stand in water. Set the plant on a pebble tray to keep the humidity up. Dry air may not only turn the leaf tips brown, but also foster a spider mite infestation.

FLOWER: It has panicles of yellow flowers, but most likely not in the house.

SIZE: This palm may be up to 8 feet tall.

PROPAGATION: Propagate by seed.

BUTTON FERN

BOTANICAL NAME: *PELLAEA ROTUNDIFOLIA*

This is an endearing small fern with little leaflets that resemble small buttons. The leaflets grow from arching fronds with dark brown stems.

LIGHT PREFERENCE: Place this fern in a medium light. An east window is best, but a north window would also work.

WATERING: This fern does not want to be kept wet, but evenly moist. Water the fern and then let the medium dry down a bit before watering again.

FLOWER: Ferns do not flower.

SIZE: It grows 6 to 12 inches tall and wide.

PROPAGATION: The fern can be divided and potted up individually.

CAPE PRIMROSE

BOTANICAL NAME: *STREPTOCARPUS*

Most often these cousins of the African violet are simply called **STREPS**. The clumps of long strappy leaves can be covered with flowers most of the year and are stunning. The flowers come in many colors and all are trumpet-shaped with a larger lip at the bottom. With the combination of colors on the flowers, they often resemble pansies.

LIGHT PREFERENCE: These grow well with African violets, as they need the same light conditions. Give them a medium light such as in an east window or grow under electric lights for 10 to 12 hours per day.

WATERING: Keep the strep evenly moist. It would be better to err on the dry side than to allow them to stand in water.

FLOWER: The flowers rise above the foliage from 8 to 12 inches. The trumpet-shaped flowers have three larger petals on the bottom fused to two smaller petals on the top. The coloring often makes them resemble pansies. There are also some cultivars with double flowers.

SIZE: These plants take up a much larger area than the typical African violet. The leaves may spread 1 foot or more.

PROPAGATION: The leaf of the strep can be used to propagate this plant in a couple of different ways. The leaf can be cut in wedges with V-shaped bottoms and placed V-shape down in a moist potting medium. The leaf can also be cut lengthwise, removing the midrib and taking each side of the leaf and laying it in the moist soil with the side that had been next to the midrib in the potting medium. Both of these procedures will result in new plants in a few weeks.

CULTIVARS: There are too many to list, but here are two easily obtained cultivars:

- **'YELLOW PINK CAP' AND 'YELLOW PURPLE CAP'**—Two newer cultivars in the gardening industry known for their two-tone flowers. Either pink or purple petals grace the top of the flower, while the lower petals are yellow.

CHINESE FAN PALM, FOUNTAIN PALM

BOTANICAL NAME: *LIVISTONA CHINENSIS*

The bright green leaves of this palm are almost completely round, unlike the more usual palm frond. These palms are a nice statement in a large room. In nature, they become quite large and form a single stem. In the home, that most likely will not occur and it will stay a many-stemmed small shrub.

LIGHT PREFERENCE: Give this palm plenty of light.

WATERING: Plant in a well-drained potting medium and keep evenly moist. Never leave it standing in water as it will rot the roots. As with most palms, dry air may encourage spider mites, so set them on pebble trays filled with water.

FLOWER: They can produce sprays of whitish-yellow flowers, but this most likely will not occur in the house.

SIZE: These palms can grow up to 50 feet tall in nature, but will not exceed 10 feet in the house.

PROPAGATION: The plant is propagated from seed.

CHINESE MONEY PLANT

BOTANICAL NAME: *PILEA PEPEROMIOIDES*

This plant has taken the houseplant world by storm in the last few years. A petiole or stem that holds up the leaf is attached in the middle of the leathery leaf, adding to its unique character. These plants are usually passed from person to person rather than being bought. Even now, they may be hard to find to purchase, but are worth the search.

LIGHT PREFERENCE: Give it a medium light as an east or west window.

WATERING: Keep this plant evenly moist and increase the humidity by placing the plant on a pebble tray with water.

FLOWER: It grows small white flowers on pinkish stems.

SIZE: The plant can grow to 12 inches high by 12 inches wide.

PROPAGATION: Offshoots are sent up from the parent an inch or two from the stem. These can be separated and potted up individually.

CROCODILE FERN

BOTANICAL NAME: *MICROSORUM MUSIFOLIUM*

The crocodile fern gets its name from the fact that the fronds resemble the skin of a crocodile. The long, wide fronds have a seer-suckered texture and are quite unique in the plant world. These are often found growing as epiphytes in their native habitat.

LIGHT PREFERENCE: A medium to bright light is best. This fern does well in an east window.

WATERING: Plant this fern in a well-drained, peat-based potting medium Keep it evenly moist, but never standing in water. Place it on a pebble tray to keep the humidity high.

FLOWER: Ferns do not flower.

SIZE: Though this fern can get 4-foot-long fronds in their native habitat, in the home they will rarely pass 2 feet.

PROPAGATION: These plants can be divided and planted up separately.

DESERT ROSE

BOTANICAL NAME: *ADENIUM OBESUM*

The large swollen stem or caudex of this plant lends to its popularity. Leaves only grow at the tip of the stems, and bright, trumpet-shaped flowers appear there as well. The flowers range in color from red to pink and white, and the plant is being hybridized for more colors. These can be found as bonsai at many garden centers. Be careful when handling these plants, as the sap can irritate the skin.

LIGHT PREFERENCE: Give this plant as much light as you have available. A south window would be best.

WATERING: Plant this succulent in a fast-draining medium. Water abundantly during the growing season, as long as there is plenty of light and warmth. When the light levels are low and it is cold, do not water much, if at all. Never water them if it is cold where they are placed, as they will rot quickly. Never let them stand in water.

FLOWER: The flowers are the main attraction of this plant, along with the swollen stems. They come in shades of red, pink, white, and combinations of all three colors. They are constantly being hybridized to come up with more colors.

SIZE: These plants can get large in their native habitat. They may be 2 to 3 feet in the house but can be kept smaller by restricting the roots like a bonsai.

PROPAGATION: These can be grown from seed and from cuttings.

ENGLISH IVY

BOTANICAL NAME: *HEDERA HELIX*

This is a popular vine, not only for its many sizes, shapes, and color combinations, but for its versatility. It can be used in a hanging basket, as a topiary, or framing a window.

LIGHT PREFERENCE: The plain-green varieties of ivy can tolerate low-light levels but prefer a medium to bright light if the plant is variegated.

WATERING: Plant your ivy in a well-drained potting medium. Water thoroughly and then allow the mix to dry slightly before watering again. Never let it stand in water. An evenly moist medium is best for the ivy. If it is allowed to get too dry, the roots may die back and be unable to take up water when it is applied. This can lead to a complete collapse of the plant. Keep the humidity high around your ivy with a pebble tray, as dry air is like a neon sign advertising to spider mites to move in. When you do water the ivy, take it to the sink and use the sink sprayer as you water, which will clean the ivy leaves and deter spider mites.

FLOWER: This plant is grown for its foliage.

SIZE: Ivy can grow long stems but can be kept under control by trimming, or train it as a wreath or other topiary shape.

PROPAGATION: Take stem cuttings and pot in moist potting medium. The stems can also be pinned to another container of potting medium while still attached to the parent. Roots will form where the stem touches the moist medium. When the roots are established, it can be cut from the parent and grown on its own.

CULTIVARS: There are so many cultivars to choose from, with many leaf types including tiny, large, green, yellow, green and yellow, green and white, and so many more. The variegated forms will need brighter light to keep the variegation. Find one, two, or three you like, make a topiary or frame a window.

- **'CURLY LOCKS'**—The solid-green leaves of this ivy are curled and twisted.

- **'GOLD BABY'**—The medium-green leaves have yellow edges.

- **'MY HEART'**—The leaves are heart shaped and dark green.

- **'SILVER DOLLAR'**—These green leaves are edged with white.

FALSE ARALIA

BOTANICAL NAME: *SCHEFFLERA ELEGANTISSIMA* 'Bianco' (formerly *DIZYGOTHECA ELEGANTISSIMA*)

This plant has an airy, fine texture as an immature plant. Each leaf has nine leaflets arranged palmately with ½-inch-wide leaflets when the plant is small, but as it matures, the leaflets may be 3 inches wide. Each leaflet has a serrated edge, adding to the character of the plant; some say that it resembles cannabis. As it matures and the leaves become larger, it becomes a statuesque architectural plant.

LIGHT PREFERENCE: Place this plant in a medium to bright light.

WATERING: Plant in a well-drained potting medium. Water thoroughly and then allow the medium to dry down a bit before watering again. Err on the side of dry rather than wet. Do not allow it to stand in water. Raise the humidity by placing the plant on a pebble tray.

FLOWER: The yellow-green flower umbels most likely will not appear in the house.

SIZE: This plant gets 25 to 50 feet in its native habitat, but is a 3- to 10-foot plant in the house.

PROPAGATION: These can be grown from seed as well as leaf and stem cuttings.

FIDDLE LEAF FIG

BOTANICAL NAME: *FICUS LYRATA*

There could not be a more popular houseplant right now. On every decorating show, every magazine spread, and countless Instagram accounts, you cannot miss this plant. Is it the plant for everyone, though? If you have soaring ceilings and the right conditions, yes. Its large, fiddle-shaped leaves and commanding presence make this a focal point in any room. This plant can be purchased in a shrub shape or tree shape, in many different sizes. The leaves are large and so collect a lot of dust. Keep them wiped clean so the plant can photosynthesize efficiently.

LIGHT PREFERENCE: Give this plant a bright light situation.

WATERING: Keep this fig evenly moist, not standing in water, but never dry either. Keep the humidity high by placing on a pebble tray.

FLOWER: Most likely it will not have flowers or fruit in the home.

SIZE: In it natural habitat, this plant can be a large tree. In the home, it can be 5 to 10 feet tall and more, if you have room.

PROPAGATION: Use stem tip cuttings or air layering.

CULTIVARS:

- **'LITTLE FIDDLE'**—A much smaller version of the larger plant with leaves that may only reach 6 to 10 inches long.

GREEN WORM FERN, E.T. FERN, GRUB FERN

BOTANICAL NAME: *POLYPODIUM FORMOSANUM*

The common names of this fern describe it perfectly. Its creeping rhizomes or modified stems resemble green worms or E.T.'s fingers. This plant is considered a "footed" fern: the airy, light green fronds arise from the green "feet."

LIGHT PREFERENCE: A medium light is best; an east window is preferable.

WATERING: Keep this fern evenly moist. If it is allowed to dry out, the fronds will begin to dry and fall off. Because of the succulent nature of the rhizomes, new fronds will grow if it is kept watered. Raise the humidity by setting the container on a pebble tray.

FLOWER: Ferns do not flower.

SIZE: The rhizomes will creep to the edges of the container, climb over the rim, and keep growing. A low, wide container is best for this creeping fern. The fronds will rise above the foliage approximately 12 to 18 inches.

PROPAGATION: Take cuttings of the rhizome with a frond attached. Pin it to a container of moist potting medium with a florist pin or piece of bent wire.

HART'S TONGUE FERN

BOTANICAL NAME: *ASPLENIUM SCOLOPENDRIUM*

This bright green fern has long, strappy fronds with wavy edges. Related to the bird's nest fern, it has a round grouping of fronds. The fronds are supposed to mimic the shape of a deer's tongue, thus the common name.

LIGHT PREFERENCE: Give this fern a medium light such as an east window.

WATERING: Keep this fern evenly moist. If it is allowed to dry out, it will lose leaves and the ends will dry out. Dry leaf tips may also occur from overly dry air. Place the fern container on a pebble tray.

FLOWER: Ferns do not flower.

SIZE: This fern will be approximately 1 foot tall.

PROPAGATION: Propagate by spores or division.

JADE PLANT

BOTANICAL NAME: *CRASSULA OVATA*

Also called a money plant or friendship plant, the jade plant is a popular houseplant and can become sizeable with bright light. It may be named "friendship plant" because of how often this plant is shared with friends. A single leaf can be the beginnings of a new plant and a friendship when you are gifted with one.

LIGHT PREFERENCE: Give the jade plant as much sun as you can. For best results, place it close to a south or west window. If it doesn't have enough light, it will have leggy, soft growth. In the winter, when the light levels are low, the times between watering will increase.

WATERING: Water thoroughly and then let it dry a bit before watering again. Do not let it completely dry out as the leaves will pucker and drop off.

FLOWER: Star-shaped white flowers appear in clusters during the short days of winter if the plant receives enough light.

SIZE: If this plant has enough light and is well cared for, it can become a large specimen, up to 5 to 6 feet.

PROPAGATION: The jade plant can be propagated from a stem cutting or a single leaf. Allow both to callus over before planting in a moist potting medium.

CULTIVARS:

- **'GOLLUM'**—This is a popular cultivar, especially with kids, as its common name is "Shrek's Ears." The rolled ends do resemble his ears, or maybe the animator made his ears resemble the plant. Who knows?

- **'VARIEGATA'**—A cultivar that appears as if white has been melted into the green, leaving faded edges instead of crisp lines. The new growth may display some pink coloration as well.

JAPANESE FATSIA

BOTANICAL NAME: *FATSIA JAPONICA* 'Spider's Web'

The large palmate leaves of this plant are striking. The fatsia can become a large plant and make a great focal point in a large area. If you have a cooler spot in the house, this plant would prefer that, so it would be a perfect plant to great your guests in a spacious foyer.

LIGHT PREFERENCE: Give it a medium to bright light to keep it more compact.

WATERING: Keep it evenly moist, reducing the amount of water in the low-light levels of winter.

FLOWER: White umbels of creamy flowers may appear, but they are unlikely in the home.

SIZE: This can become a large houseplant, 5 to 6 feet tall.

PROPAGATION: Propagate from stem cuttings, but the large leaves may need to be cut in half to prevent the cutting from losing too much water as it roots. It may also be air layered.

KANGAROO FERN

BOTANICAL NAME: *MICROSORUM DIVERSIFOLIUM*

This "footed" fern is different in that its rhizomes aren't overly fuzzy and are a dark chocolate color. The bright green fronds are deeply lobed. It's usually offered as a hanging basket; the rhizomes will keep growing until they spill over the rim and down the side of the container. They can completely cover the pot if allowed, or it can be moved into a wider pot. A low, wide pot is the best container for this fern.

LIGHT PREFERENCE: As with most ferns, it would like a medium light; an east window is perfect.

WATERING: Do not let this fern dry out, but keep it evenly moist and never wet. If allowed to dry out, the result will be yellow leaves that will fall off. It is a little forgiving because the rhizomes hold a bit of water. Keep the humidity up by placing the container on a pebble tray.

FLOWER: Ferns do not flower.

SIZE: The fronds rise above the rhizomes approximately 1 foot. The plant will spread as wide as the container it is in and beyond.

PROPAGATION: Remove a piece of the rhizome with a frond intact and pin it to a moist potting medium.

NERVE PLANT, MOSAIC PLANT, SILVER NET PLANT

BOTANICAL NAME: *FITTONIA*

The nerve plant is grown because of its heavily veined leaves. Because they have thin leaves that prefer high humidity, a terrarium is a perfect environment. They come in pink, white, green, and red, and some even have pie-crust edges. This endearing plant is also used often as a fairy garden plant.

LIGHT PREFERENCE: Medium light is best. High light will burn the leaves.

WATERING: This plant does not want to be too wet, as it will rot. On the other hand, do not allow it to dry out as it will drop its leaves. Keep it evenly moist. This plant loves high humidity, so place on a pebble tray or in a terrarium.

FLOWER: It is grown for its beautiful foliage. If flower spikes appear, cut them off so all the energy can be used for the foliage.

SIZE: This is a low-growing groundcover up to 4 to 5 inches tall.

PROPAGATION: Tip cuttings root easily in moist potting medium.

CULTIVARS:

• **'WHITE ANNE'**—This cultivar has green leaves with bright white veins.

• **'RED ANNE'**—It has green leaves with red veins.

• **'PINK STAR'**—It has green, ruffled leaves with pink veins.

PIN STRIPE CALATHEA

BOTANICAL NAME: *CALATHEA ORNATA*

The beautiful foliage of this plant is its main attraction. It is often thought to be a prayer plant, and they are related. On the dark green leaves, pink stripes feather out from the midrib to the edges on a slight curve. The undersides of the leaves are burgundy.

LIGHT PREFERENCE: Calatheas prefer a medium exposure to ensure the stripes stay a bright pink. Direct sun will fade the markings, yet too dark an exposure will not allow them to stay bright.

WATERING: Keep it evenly moist, not wet, but never dry. Place on a pebble tray to keep the humidity high. This is a must, as the leaf edges will turn brown if grown in dry air.

FLOWER: These plants are grown for their beautiful foliage and most likely won't flower in the house.

SIZE: It may grow to 2 feet tall.

PROPAGATION: The calathea can be propagated by division.

STAGHORN FERN

BOTANICAL NAME: *PLATYCERIUM BIFURCATUM*

This epiphytic fern has an imposing presence because of it large, antler-like fronds. These gray-green fronds rise out of non-fertile fronds and fork at the ends, giving them the appearance of antlers. The "antlers" are the fertile fronds, as they will produce the spores that can be used to propagate more ferns. The brown, papery, non-fertile fronds are the shield fronds that shield the roots that hold them tight to the trees they grow on. Staghorns are sold as small potted plants and often already mounted on a piece of wood, ready to hang on the wall like a mounted trophy. The brown fronds are often mistaken for dead parts of the plant, but they are not dead and should not be removed.

LIGHT PREFERENCE: As these naturally grow on trees, they are used to a dappled light, but not full sun. Give them a medium to bright light with no direct sun.

WATERING: Take your plant to the sink or shower and let the water flow on the rootball to ensure the potting medium or moss is completely soaked. Spray the green fronds as well. This may need to be done once a week or more if the fern is in a bright light. Do not allow them to dry out. If there is a place in the kitchen or bathroom for your fern with good light, they would appreciate the added humidity.

FLOWER: Ferns do not produce flowers.

SIZE: These can become sizeable plants. If the shield fronds cover the piece of wood they are on, attach the wood they are growing on to a larger piece of wood.

PROPAGATION: They can be propagated by spores or by removing the smaller plants off the large parent plant.

Index

LISA ELDRED STEINKOPF is the Houseplant Guru, who features all things houseplants on her blog, www.thehouseplantguru.com. She grew up in rural mid-Michigan, where being immersed in nature every day nurtured her love for the outdoors, especially plants. Living down the road from her grandma meant spending a lot of time watching her lavish attention to her African violets and other houseplants. This is where the love for them began. Being an avid outdoor gardener as well has led Lisa to writing a monthly column and frequent articles for *Michigan Gardening* and *Michigan Gardener* magazines, respectively. In addition, she has written for HGTVgardens.com, *Real Simple* magazine, and the houseplant section of Allan Armitage's Greatest Perennials and Annuals app. Lisa has worked for over a decade as the annuals and houseplants manager at Steinkopf Nursery, and has been interviewed online, in print, and on TV about houseplants. She is a member of numerous plant groups, including the Michigan Cactus and Succulent Society, the Town and Country African Violet Society, and the Hardy Plant Society. She cares for over 1,000 houseplants in her home in the Detroit area, where she lives with her husband, John. Lisa feels that every home, office, and apartment should have a houseplant, and there is a houseplant for every situation. A green thumb is something everyone can have!